13 May 1984

Happy Mother's Day, LaVerne —

Love — The Lampi's

—A MAVERICK PUBLICATION—

THE ALL NATURAL SOUP BOOK

by
Darcy Williamson

MAVERICK PUBLICATIONS
DRAWER 5007 • BEND, OREGON 97708

Cover Photo

by

John Allgair

Copyright © 1982, Darcy Williamson

All rights reserved. No part of the material protected by this copyright notice may be reproduced or utilized in any form or by any means, electronic or mechanical, including photocopying, recording, or by any informational storage and retrieval system without written permission from the copyright owner. Printed in the United States of America.

*Special thanks to Cynthia McCure
for the use of her stove and warm hospitality.*

Table of Contents

	Page
Introduction	1
Bouillon, Broth and Stock	3
Chilled Soups	11
Chowders	25
Creamed Soups	37
Fruit Soups	57
Main Dish Soups	67
Vegetable Soups	86
Dumplings, Noodles, Crackers and Toppings	115
Index	127

Introduction

Chicken soup is reputed to have mysterious healing qualities, especially in instances involving common colds, flu and fatigue. What a miracle, chicken. Right? Wrong. The miracle lies not in the chicken, but in the soup. Would mushroom or vegetable soup produce such "healing qualities"? Certainly! For a soup's major purpose is to improve digestion and stimulate appetite by introducing a deliciously flavored liquid to the system, increasing the flow of digestive juices. But that's not all! Soup adds a variety of nutrients to a meal which may not have otherwise been assimilated. Now, let's take a look at an ailing, wheezing, stuffed-up, nauseous individual. Would such a person eagerly dig into a heavy four course meal? Or would that person be more apt to sip a steaming mug of nourishing soup?

Now that the healthful properties of soup have been established, doesn't it stand to reason that a soup made fresh with natural ingredients rates far above one dumped from a can? One which is not heavy in sodium, sugar (Yep! Read the label!), M.S.G., artificial flavorings and additives?

Natural soups are not only nutritious but versitile, as well. They can be served hot or chilled; accompanying a meal; the main portion of the meal; or as a dessert (fruit soups)! And what a practical way to use yesterday's leftover cooked vegetables, rice or potatoes? When soup is regularly prepared and served, little, if any, food is wasted.

Chapter 1

Bouillon, Broth and Stock

Stocks are the foundation of many soups. Though recipes throughout this book may suggest a certain stock, broth or bouillon, do not allow that to influence your own inventiveness. If you have been frugal by saving your potato and carrot peelings, green pepper seeds, apple cores, mushroom stems, or what have you, for use in making your own soup base, by all means use it! Your stock invention is bound to be teaming with nutrients which may otherwise have been discarded.

When making your own stock, keep in mind that anything goes—almost. That tomato worm is disqualified due to the fact that this book is dedicated to vegetarian cooking. But cabbage cores, leftover cooked grains, outer leaves of cauliflower, and garden herbs can all be tossed into the stock pot. Add sufficient liquid such as water, fluid left from steaming vegetables or sprouting seeds, or liquid drained from soaked legumes (provided you washed the beans first). Since stock should simmer two to three hours, a pot with a tight fitting lid is essential.

After you have carefully strained your stock (I've found pouring stock through several layers of cheese cloth a simple method), discard solids. Vegetable stock forms no layer of fat on its surface to help seal in freshness. Therefore, it is important to use it within a day or two. Of course this is not always practical. Freezing your soup base is an excellent alternative, since frozen stock will keep up to six months. When freezing, allow an inch of air space for expansion.

The following recipe can be added to any stock, bouillon or soup base to give it extra flavor. You may wish to substitute some of the herbs to suit your own taste. Or you may prefer to scrap my recipe in favor of your own concoction.

Kitchen Bouquet

1 Tbsp. dried parsley leaves
1 Tbsp. dried celery leaves
2 tsp. dried thyme leaves
1 tsp. dried sage leaves
½ tsp. savory
2 bay leaves
1 clove
2 tsp. dried chives

Mix herbs together. Place herbs in square of cheese cloth and tie securely. Dangle sachet, by sturdy thread or string, in simmering stock or soup during the final 10 minutes of cooking. Remove herbs and discard.

Dry soup mix is another recipe easily altered to your own taste. The addition of brewer's yeast or fresh wheat germ can easily be added to the mix. The flavor possibilities are as wide as your imagination. Here's a mix which may help spur your inventiveness:

Dry Soup Mix

1 cup dry milk powder
1 cup soy flour
1 cup finely ground barley
¼ cup dried parsley
3 Tbsp. powdered kelp
1 Tbsp. dried thyme
1 Tbsp. dried basil
¼ tsp. cayenne pepper

Combine all ingredients and store in tightly covered container. Use 3 Tbsp. mix to each cup of liquid.

Bran Broth (4 servings)

2 cups red wheat bran
3 cups cold water
1 tsp. vegetable salt (optional)

Soak bran in salted water overnight. Strain. Heat broth thoroughly before serving, but do not allow to boil.

Carrot-Spinach Broth (serves 4)

6 carrots
1 bunch parsley
4 comfrey leaves
2 cups chopped celery (leaves included, of course)
½ lb. chopped fresh spinach
½ tsp. vegetable salt (optional)
4 cups water

Put all ingredients in blender container and run until vegetables are coarsley chopped. Pour into saucepan, cover and simmer 35 minutes. Strain broth.

Carrot-Turnip Stock (1 qt.)

2 cups grated carrots
2 cups grated turnips
1 medium onion, diced
¼ cup fresh parsley sprigs
½ tsp. dried thyme
½ tsp. savory
2 tsp. vegetable salt (optional)
1 qt. water

Put ingredients in large pot; cover tightly and simmer gently 30 minutes. Cool. Strain.

Clear Mushroom Stock (2 qts.)

2 lbs. mushrooms, finely chopped
2 qts. water
½ tsp. vegetable salt (optional)
1 Tbsp. Tamari soy sauce

Simmer mushrooms in water for 2 hours in covered saucepan. Remove from heat and allow to stand for 3 hours. Strain, pressing pulp dry. Discard pulp. Add remaining ingredients and heat once again.

Miso Broth (serves 4)

4 cups mushroom broth
¼ cup white miso (fermented soybean paste)
¼ tsp. vegetable salt (optional)
1 egg, beaten
2 tsp. sweet rice wine (optional)
Twists of lemon peel
Slices of green onion tops

Bring broth, mixed with miso and salt, to a boil. While swirling soup in pan, gradually trickle in beaten egg. Remove from heat and add wine. Place a twist of lemon in each bowl before adding soup. Top with green onion.

Mushroom Broth (4 servings)
(good with Farina Dumplings)

    3 lbs. mushrooms, chopped
    1½ qts. cold water
    2 cups grated carrots
    1 medium onion, chopped
    1 turnip, chopped
    ½ cup chopped celery leaves
    2 cloves garlic, crushed
    2 bay leaves
    1 Tbsp. chopped savory
    4 peppercorns, crushed
    ¼ tsp. herb or vegetable salt (optional)

Combine all ingredients in large saucepan and bring to boiling. Reduce heat. Cover and simmer 2 hours. Strain, squeezing or pressing solids to extract moisture from mushrooms. Discard solids.

Onion-Garlic Broth (2 qts.)

    1 lb. onions, sliced
    8 cloves garlic, halved
    1 spring dill
    2 bay leaves
    1 tsp. vegetable salt (optional)
    2 qts. water

Combine ingredients in large saucepan or kettle. Cover and simmer 40 minutes. Keep cover on kettle and allow broth to cool. Strain. Discard solids.

Potato-Vegetable Bouillon (2 qts.)

2½ qts. water
1 lb. potatoes, thinly sliced
2 medium onions, chopped
1½ cups chopped celery
2 carrots, shredded
3 ripe tomatoes, diced
½ tsp. sea salt (optional)
¼ cup chopped parsley
½ tsp. dried thyme
1 bay leaf

Combine all ingredients in kettle and bring to boiling over medium heat. Simmer 1½ hours. Put bouillon through fine strainer. Discard spent vegetables.

Rich Vegetable Broth (serves 4)

2 Tbsp. butter
2 Tbsp. soy powder
½ cup brewer's yeast
4 vegetable bouillon cubes, crushed
1 clove garlic, crushed
4 cups water

Blend butter with soy powder, yeast, bouillon and garlic. Stir into water. Heat to boiling. Strain, if desired.

Tomato Bouillon (1½ qts.)

6 cups tomato juice
1 bay leaf
½ cup minced celery
½ cup chopped fennel
4 cloves
2 Tbsp. fresh basil
1½ cups minced onion
1 tsp. vegetable salt (optional)

Combine tomato juice, bay leaf, celery, fennel, cloves, basil, onion and salt. Bring to boiling, reduce heat and simmer 5 to 7 minutes. Strain.

Vegetable Bouillon (1 to 1½ qts.)

1½ qts. water
¾ cup dry white wine
½ cup minced celery
½ cup chopped onion
⅔ cup shredded carrot
½ cup minced mushrooms
¼ cup chopped parsley
2 Tbsp. chopped fresh thyme
2 Tbsp. chopped fresh tarragon leaves
3 crushed peppercorns
2 cloves garlic, crushed
¼ tsp. vegetable salt (optional)

Combine all ingredients in saucepan and bring to boiling. Cover, lower heat and simmer 1 hour. Strain, discarding solids. Refrigerate in covered jars.

Vegetable Soup Base (1½ qts.)

2 cups tomato juice
2 cups carrot juice
2 crushed garlic cloves
2 Tbsp. onion juice
1 cup chopped parsley
2 cups water
1 tsp. vegetable salt (optional)
½ tsp. celery seed

Put all ingredients in blender container and run at high speed 15 to 20 seconds. Chill or freeze until needed as a soup base.

Vegetable Stock (1 qt.)

1 qt. water
1 cup shredded carrot
1 ripe tomato, diced
½ cup diced turnip
½ cup diced celery
½ cup minced fresh parsley soup
½ cup chopped watercress
3 cloves garlic, crushed
1½ tsp. Tamari soy sauce
2 crushed peppercorns

Combine ingredients in saucepan and bring to boiling. Reduce heat, cover and simmer 2 hours. Strain; discard solids.

Chapter 2

Chilled Soups

Beet-Potato Soup (6 servings)

1 cup sliced, cooked beets
½ cup sliced onion
½ tsp. vegetable salt (optional)
2 Tbsp. freshly squeezed lemon juice
1 medium-sized boiled potato, sliced
1 cup carrot juice
1 cup yogurt

Combine all ingredients in blender container and puree (or use a food mill to puree ingredients if a blender or electricity is not available). Chill.

Chard and Lentil Soup (serves 6)

2½ lbs. Swiss chard, chopped
1½ cups lentils
½ cup olive oil
1 medium-sized onion, chopped
4 garlic cloves, minced
½ cup chopped celery
¾ cup freshly squeezed lemon juice
1 cup yogurt

Cover lentil with cold water and cook in covered kettle until tender. Add chard to lentils and continue cooking 10 minutes. Saute' onion, garlic and celery in olive oil until tender. Stir into soup, along with lemon juice. Chill. Stir in yogurt just before serving.

Chilled Chickweed-Nettle Soup (4 servings)

2 Tbsp. butter, melted
2 Tbsp. whole wheat flour
½ tsp. granulated garlic
1½ cups raw milk
½ cup yogurt
3 cups fresh chickweed
1 cup stinging nettle greens

In blender, along with ½ cup milk, puree chickweed and nettles. Blend melted butter, flour and granulated garlic together, then add 1 cup milk. Cook over medium heat, stirring, until mixture thickens. Add pureed greens. Cover and cook slowly over medium-low heat 15 minutes. Do not allow to come to complete boil. Chill.

Chilled Cream of Tomato Soup (serves 2)

2 cups tomato juice
1 cup raw milk
½ tsp. honey
¼ tsp. sea salt (optional)
½ tsp. crushed celery seed
2 tsp. grated onion
1 tsp. Tamari soy sauce

Combine ingredients. Mix well. Chill.

Chilled Curried Soup (serves 4)

1 Tbsp. butter
1 medium-sized onion, chopped
1 medium-sized apple, cored and diced
1 medium-sized potato, diced
2 stalks celery, chopped
2 cups Vegetable Stock (page 10)
1½ tsp. curry powder
1 cup yogurt
1 tsp. honey
Lemon slices

Melt butter in large saucepan over medium heat. Add onion, apple, potato and celery. Stir in broth and curry powder. Cover and simmer gently 25 minutes, stirring occassionally. Cool slightly. Puree in food mill or blender. Chill thoroughly. At serving time, combine yogurt with honey. Blend with soup and serve in chilled bowls. Garnish with lemon slices.

Chilled Herb Soup (6 servings)

1½ qts. Tomato Bouillon (page 9)
1 head lettuce, torn into pieces
1 bunch watercress
1 bunch parsley
¼ tsp. chopped chives
2 tsp. chopped chervil
3 Tbsp. brewer's yeast (optional)
1 egg yolk
1 cup yogurt

In blender container, combine all ingredients, except yogurt, and blend smooth. Chill. Just before serving, stir yogurt into chilled soup.

Chilled Minestrone (serves 6)

1 qt. Carrot-Turnip Stock (page 5)
2 cups fresh tomato juice
2 cups carrot juice
1 potato, cubed
1 carrot, grated
½ lb. Swiss chard, torn
1 medium-sized zucchini, sliced
3 leeks, cut lengthwise
½ cup whole wheat pasta

Combine stock, juices, potato and carrot. Simmer in covered kettle 20 minutes. Add remaining ingredients and simmer, uncovered, 10 minutes or until pasta is tender. Chill.

Chilled Salad Soup (8 servings)

1 envelope unflavored gelatin
2 tsp. honey
1 tsp. vegetable salt (optional)
1½ cups water
2 lb. ripe tomatoes, chopped
¼ cup safflower oil
2 Tbsp. freshly squeezed lemon juice
1 small cucumber, thinly sliced
1 medium-sized green pepper, diced
2 carrots, grated
1 bunch radishes, sliced
¼ cup minced onion
3 hard-cooked eggs, chopped

Mix gelatin, honey and salt in saucepan. Stir in water. Heat, Stirring, until gelatin dissolves. Beat into remaining ingredients. Chill, stirring occasionally, until slightly thickened. Serve in chilled bowls.

Chilled Spanish Soup (6 servings)
1 cup vine-ripped tomatoes, chopped
½ cup minced green pepper
½ cup minced cucumber
½ cup minced onion
½ cup minced celery
¼ cup minced parsley
1 clove garlic, crushed
1 Tbsp. cider vinegar
2 Tbsp. olive oil
¼ tsp. sea salt (optional)
2 cups tomato juice

Combine all ingredients and mix well. Cover and chill at least 12 hours. Serve in small chilled bowls.

Chilled Split Pea and Mint Soup (8 servings)

1½ cup split peas
4 cups water
4 cups Rich Vegetable Broth (page 8)
1 medium onion, minced
2 cloves garlic, crushed
2 fresh sprigs mint
½ tsp. sea salt (optional)
2 cups yogurt

Bring peas and water to boiling. Remove from heat and allow to stand 1 hour. Add broth, onion, garlic, mint and salt. Cover and simmer until peas are tender. Cool slightly, then puree in blender or food mill. Chill overnight. When ready to serve, stir yogurt into soup.

Coconut Soup (6 servings)

1 qt. Bran Broth (page 5)
1 cup raw milk
1 coconut (meat cut into chunks) and liquid
¼ cup soy powder
3 Tbsp. freshly squeezed lemon juice
2 tsp. grated lemon rind
1 cup alfalfa sprouts

Combine all ingredients, except sprouts, in blender container and blend until smooth. Garnish chilled soup with sprouts.

Cold Cucumber-Potato Soup (4 servings)

¼ cup butter
1 cup sliced leeks
3 cucumbers, diced
2 cups water
1 pt. carrot juice
2 cups thinly sliced potatoes
Vegetable salt to taste (optional)
Dash nutmeg

Melt butter in pan; add leeks and cook until tender. Add cucumbers and water. Boil, covered, 5 minutes. Add juice and potatoes. Cook until tender. Press through sieve, then beat with whisk. Season to taste. Chill.

Cold Tomato-Yogurt Soup (2 servings)

2½ cups fresh tomato puree
1 cup yogurt
2 Tbsp. minced parsley
1 Tbsp. minced fresh basil
Lemon slices

Combine all ingredients, except lemon slices. Mix well. Chill. Garnish servings with a slice of lemon.

Cream of Almond Soup (4 servings)

2 large cucumbers, sliced
3 onions, sliced
2 cups carrot juice
⅔ cup blanched almonds, ground
½ cup yogurt
⅓ cup slivered almonds

Simmer cucumbers and onion in juice 10 minutes. Season to taste. Press through sieve. Chill. Stir in ground almonds and yogurt. Serve at once garnished with slivered almonds.

Cream of Avocado Soup (6 servings)

3 avocado, halved and peeled
1 cup Vegetable Bouillon (page 9)
3 cups yogurt
½ tsp. vegetable salt (optional)
½ tsp. vegetable salt (optional)
2 tsp. freshly squeezed lemon juice
1 Tbsp. fresh mint, minced

Place all ingredients in blender container and puree. Chill before servings.

Cucumber and Mint Soup (5 servings)

4 medium-sized cucumbers, sliced
8 green onions, sliced
3 cups water
½ tsp. sea salt (optional)
6 Tbsp. arrowroot
¼ cup chopped mint
1½ cups yogurt

Combine cucumbers, onion, water and salt. Simmer until vegetables are tender-crisp. Mix arrowroot with small amount of cold water. Stir into soup. Cook, stirring, until soup thickens. Remove from heat, puree soup. Chill. Add mint and yogurt. Stir until blended.

Iced Borsch (4 servings)

1 lb. cooked beets, sliced
½ cup beet juice
1 medium-sized onion, quartered
1 Tbsp. minced fresh dill
1 cup carrot juice
½ tsp. vegetable salt (optional)
2 Tbsp. cider vinegar
½ tsp. dried tarragon
1 cup yogurt
4 hard-cooked eggs, sliced

In blender, mix beets, beet juice, onion and dill. Transfer mixture to bowl and add carrot juice, salt, vinegar and tarragon. Stir in yogurt. Chill. Serve garnished with hard-cooked egg slices.

Iced Broccoli Soup (6 servings)

1 lb. broccoli, diced
1 qt. Clear Mushroom Stock (page 6)
1 medium-sized onion, chopped
½ cup chopped celery
¼ cup chopped parsley
1 cup grated carrot
2 Tbsp. arrowroot starch
½ tsp. vegetable salt (optional)
Dash cayenne
1 cup yogurt

Combine broccoli, stock, onion, celery, parsley, carrot, salt and cayenne. Simmer 15 minutes. Add arrowroot mixed with a little cold water. Simmer and stir until thick. Cool slightly. Puree in blender. Chill at least 5 hours. Stir in yogurt just before serving.

Indian Curry Soup (5 to 6 servings)

1 medium-sized onion, minced
2 apples, sliced
2 Tbsp. butter
2 Tbsp. curry powder
½ cup whole wheat flour
Dash cayenne pepper
3½ cups Carrot-Spinach Broth (page 5)
1½ cups yogurt
¼ tsp. chili powder

Cook onion and apple in butter until tender. Add curry and cook for a few minutes. Stir in flour and cayenne. Add broth slowly and bring to boiling. Remove from heat. Cool. Rub through sieve and chill. Stir chili powder into yogurt. Stir yogurt mixture into chilled soup just before serving.

Jellied Consommé (serves 5 to 6)

3½ cups boiling water
4 vegetable bouillon cubes
2 envelopes unflavored gelatin
¼ cup cold water
2 parsley sprigs
2 stalks celery, diced
1 tsp. honey
1 clove garlic, crushed
Dash cayenne
2 cloves
1 Tbsp. cider vinegar
Lemon slices

Dissolve bouillon in boiling water. Combine bouillon with parsley, celery, honey, garlic, cayenne and cloves. Bring to a boil. Simmer 20 minutes. Strain.
Soften gelatin in cold water; stir into hot soup, add vinegar. Chill in refrigerator. Garnish with lemon slices.

Jellied Tomato Soup (4 servings)

2 cups chopped vine-ripened tomatoes
½ cup diced carrots
¼ cup diced onion
¼ cup chopped celery leaves
1 cup water
½ tsp. vegetable salt (optional)
Dash cayenne
3 cloves
1 bay leaf
3 sprigs fresh thyme
1 Tbsp. unflavored gelatin
¼ cup water
½ cup minced parsley

Combine first 10 ingredients in saucepan and bring to boiling over medium heat. Reduce to simmering and cook, covered, 30 minutes. Strain. Measure 2 cups hot soup.

Soften gelatin in cold water, then stir into hot soup. Pour into shallow pan and chill until firm. Cut into cubes and pile into small soup bowls. Top with chopped parsley.

Jellied Vegetable Soup (4 servings)

2 envelopes unflavored gelatin
½ cup carrot juice
¾ cup boiling Vegetable Stock (page 10)
1 cup cold Vegetable Stock
¼ cup freshly squeezed lemon juice
1 Tbsp. honey
½ cup diced raw carrots
½ cup fresh raw peas
¼ cup minced celery
2 Tbsp. chopped chives or parsley

Sprinkle gelatin over carrot juice to soften. Combine with boiling stock and stir until gelatin has dissolved. Add cold stock, lemon juice and honey. Chill until mixture is partially set. Stir in carrots, peas and celery. Transfer to shallow, wet pan. Chill. When mixture is firm, scramble coarsely with fork. Spoon into chilled bowls and sprinkle with chives or parsley.

Lemon Tree Soup (6 servings)

3 avocado
¾ cup freshly squeezed lemon juice
3 cups Vegetable Bouillon (page 9)
1½ cups yogurt
1 tsp. vegetable salt (optional)

Puree avocado with lemon juice and bouillon. Add half of the yogurt and salt. Chill thoroughly. Garnish with remaining yogurt.

Senegalese Soup (serves 4)

1/2 cup butter
1 1/2 cups chopped onion
1/2 cup shredded carrot
1/2 cup diced celery
1 1/2 cups grated tart apple
2 Tbsp. curry powder
2 Tbsp. whole wheat flour
3 1/2 cups Vegetable Soup Base (page 10)
4 egg yolks
1 1/2 cups yogurt
2 tsp. freshly squeezed lemon juice
1/2 cup grated coconut

Saute' vegetables and apple in butter until vegetables are tender. Stir in flour and curry powder. Cook a few minutes. Force through sieve. Gradually stir in soup base. Bring to boiling. Reduce heat, cover and simmer 15 minutes.

In medium-sized bowl, beat egg yolks slightly. Beat in yogurt. Gradually stir into soup mixture. Cook over medium heat, stirring, until mixture thickens. Remove from heat. Stir in lemon juice. Cool. Chill.

Serve in chilled bowls with coconut sprinkled over soup.

Sour Milk Soup (serves 6 to 8)

4 cups sour milk
2 cups cream
1/2 cup cider vinegar
1 1/2 cups cooked beet tops, chopped
Few springs of fresh dill, chopped
2 cucumbers, diced
4 hard-cooked eggs, chopped
1/2 tsp. vegetable salt (optional)
Ice cubes

Beat sour milk and cream separately until bubbles appear on surface. Combine cream with milk. Add vinegar, beet tops, dill and cucumbers. Mix well. Add egg. Place a couple of ice cubes in each bowl before adding soup. Serve at once.

Spinach-Avocado Soup (6 servings)

1½ cups cooked, drained spinach
2 avocado, halved and peeled
1¼ cups Vegetable Bouillon (page 9)
1 cup yogurt
¼ tsp. vegetable salt
¼ tsp. grated lemon peel
3 Tbsp. freshly squeezed lemon juice
1 hard-cooked egg, sieved

Puree avocado with spinach. Blend with remaining ingredients (except egg). Cover. Chill thoroughly. Garnish with sieved egg.

Tomato-Pea Soup (serves 4)

2 cups cooked fresh peas
1½ cups boiling Onion-Garlic Broth (page 7)
½ cup minced onion
2 tsp. chopped fresh dill
1 cup yogurt
1 vine-ripened tomato, diced

Combine peas, broth, onion and dill in blender container. Liquefy. Chill. Just before serving, stir in yogurt. Top with diced tomato.

Watercress-Avocado Soup (6 servings)

2 avocado, halved and peeled
2 cups watercress sprigs
1½ cups Vegetable Bouillon (page 9)
1 cup yogurt
½ tsp. vegetable salt (optional)
1 tsp. grated onion
2 tsp. freshly squeezed lemon juice

Puree avocado with watercress and bouillon. Mix in yogurt, salt, onion and lemon juice. Chill thoroughly.

Yogurt-Cucumber Soup (6 servings)

1 pint yogurt
3 medium-sized cucumbers, grated
2 Tbsp. freshly squeezed lemon juice
1 tsp. grated lemon rind
2 tsp. fresh dill
2 cloves garlic, crushed
2 tsp. powdered milk
2 Tbsp. sunflower oil
1 tsp. dill seeds
2 Tbsp. fresh mint

Place all ingredients in blender container and blend until smooth. Chill. Great with whole wheat crackers!

Chapter 3

Chowders

Asparagus Chowder (3 to 4 servings)

3 cups cut-up asparagus, cooked
1 cup buttermilk
2 vegetable bouillon cubes
1½ cups hot water
1 tsp. chili powder
¼ tsp. cumin

Combine ingredients in blender container and blend smooth. Pour into saucepan and heat. Do not boil.

Autumn Vegetable Chowder (5 to 6 servings)

¼ cup butter
1 medium onion, chopped
2 carrots, grated
2 potatoes, diced
½ cup minced celery leaves
3 ripe tomatoes, chopped
3 Tbsp. Dry Soup Mix (page 4)
1 cup carrot juice
1 Tbsp. Tamari soy sauce
2 cups raw milk
2½ cups shredded natural Cheddar cheese

Melt butter in kettle; add onion, carrots and celery leaves. Cook until onion is limp. Add potatoes, tomatoes, Dry Soup Mix, carrot juice and Tamari. Cover and simmer 25 minutes, stirring occasionally. Stir in milk and cheese. Heat until cheese has melted. Serve at once.

Celery Chowder (serves 6)

4 cups cooked diced celery
1 medium onion, minced
1 tsp. celery seed
1 clove garlic, crushed
1 cup cooked diced carrots
2 Tbsp. butter
1 Tbsp. whole wheat flour
½ tsp. vegetable salt (optional)
Dash cayenne pepper
3 cups raw milk, scalded
2 egg yolks, beaten

Rub celery through a sieve. Saute' onion, celery seed, garlic and carrots in butter for 5 minutes. Blend in flour, salt and cayenne. Add milk, gradually, stirring constantly. Heat to boiling, add egg yolks and cook 2 minutes. Serve at once.

Cheese Chowder (5 to 6 servings)

3 Tbsp. peanut oil
½ cup chopped celery
½ cup grated carrots
½ cup chopped onion
1 Tbsp. whole wheat flour
½ cup powdered milk solids
1 cup hot Vegetable Bouillon (page 9)
2½ cups raw milk
1 cup grated natural Cheddar cheese

Saute' vegetables lightly in oil. Mix together flour and milk powder. Sprinkle over vegetables. Add bouillon and mix well. Gradually add milk and cook over medium heat until slightly thickened. Add cheese and stir until cheese has melted. Serve at once.

Corn and Cheese Chowder (serves 6)

Corn scraped from 6 ears
3 cups boiling water
2 vegetable bouillon cubes
4 cups grated potatoes
1½ cups chopped onion
1 cup chopped celery
Dash cayenne
½ cup raw milk
½ cup grated natural Cheddar cheese

Combine ingredients, except milk and cheese, and simmer 25 minutes. Add milk and cheese. Heat and stir until cheese melts.

Corn Chowder (4 servings)

3 Tbsp. butter
½ tsp. vegetable salt (optional)
1 medium onion, diced
4 medium potatoes, diced
2 cups water
3 slices whole wheat bread
2 cups raw milk
2 cups fresh corn, cooked

Melt butter in kettle. Add salt and onion. Saute' until onion is lightly browned. Add potatoes and water. Cook until potatoes are tender.

Soak bread in milk. Add corn and bread-milk mixture to cooked potato mixture. Heat to boiling. Serve at once.

Corn-Tomato Chowder (6 to 8 servings)

1 onion, minced
2 Tbsp. butter
2½ cups corn cut from cob
2 cups diced potatoes
1½ cups ripe tomatoes, diced
½ tsp. sea salt (optional)
1 Tbsp. honey
2 cups carrot juice
2 cups boiling water
1 cup cream

Saute' onion in butter 5 minutes. Add vegetables, salt, honey, juice and water. Simmer gently 45 minutes or until potatoes are tender. Stir in cream. Serve at once.

Dried Corn Chowder (3 to 4 servings)

1 cup dried corn
2 Tbsp. butter
3 Tbsp. minced onion
½ cup chopped celery
3 Tbsp. minced green pepper
1 cup grated raw potato
2 cups water
½ tsp. sea salt (optional)
¼ tsp. paprika
1 bay leaf
3 Tbsp. whole wheat flour
½ cup yogurt
1½ cups raw milk, hot

Cover corn with water and allow to soak overnight. Cook corn in soaking liquid until tender (approximately 2 hours). Drain. Saute' onion, celery and green pepper in butter for 5 minutes. Add potato, water, salt, paprika, bay and corn. Simmer 45 minutes. Stir flour into yogurt. Add milk to yogurt-flour mixture, then stir slowly into simmering soup. Serve at once.

Fiddlehead Chowder (3 to 4 servings)

1 qt. fiddleheads (furled Ostrich ferns), cut into ½" pieces
2 cups celery, diced
1 green pepper, diced
½ cup onion, chopped
¼ cup butter
1 large ripe tomato, chopped
¼ tsp. sea salt (optional)
½ tsp. honey
¼ tsp. paprika
4 cups boiling water

    Saute' fiddleheads, celery, green pepper and onion in butter 5 minutes. Add tomatoes and boiling water along with sauteed vegetables and seasoning. Cover and simmer gently 45 minutes.

Green Chili and Corn Chowder (serves 6)

1 Tbsp. butter
2 cloves garlic, crushed
½ cup chopped onion
2 stalks celery, thinly sliced
2 cups left-over mashed potatoes
5 cups raw milk
2 cups cooked corn kernels
1 large mild green chili, chopped
1 tsp. oregano leaves
Shredded Cheddar cheese
Sliced green onion

    Saute' garlic, onion and celery in butter. Cook until onion is limp. Add mashed potatoes and milk. Stir in corn, chilies and oregano. Cover and simmer 15 minutes. Season to taste. Ladle soup into bowls and add cheese and onion.

Lima Bean Chowder (4 servings)

1 cup dried lima beans
3 cups boiling water
½ tsp. sea salt (optional)
½ cup diced celery
1 carrot, grated
¼ cup minced green pepper
1 onion, minced
3 Tbsp. butter
2 Tbsp. whole wheat flour
1½ cups raw milk
Cayenne pepper to taste

Combine beans with water in kettle and boil 2 minutes. Remove from heat and allow beans to soak 4 hours. Add salt and bring to boiling. Reduce heat and simmer 45 minutes. Add celery, carrot and green pepper. Continue cooking 15 minutes.

Melt butter in skillet. Add onion and saute' until tender. Stir in flour and slowly add milk; cook stirring until smooth. Add to lima bean mixture. Cook until slightly thickened. Season to taste with cayenne and additional salt, if desired.

New England Vegetable Chowder (5 servings)

¼ cup butter
1 cup diced celery
1 cup diced carrot
3 Tbsp. green onion
2 cups fresh corn kernels
½ cup water
½ tsp. sea salt (optional)
4 cups raw milk
1 cup raw peas
¼ cup chopped parsley
Grated natural Cheddar cheese

Melt butter in heavy saucepan; add celery, carrot, onion, corn, water and salt. Cover and cook 45 minutes. Add milk and peas; heat. Sprinkle with parsley. Sprinkle cheese over soup just before serving.

Oatmeal Chowder (4 servings)

3 **Tbsp. butter**
1 **onion, diced**
3 **carrots, grated**
2 **large vine-ripened tomatoes, diced**
1 **cup cooked legumes**
2 **cups cooked rolled oats**
1 **qt. water**
¼ **tsp. sea salt** (optional)

Brown onion in butter. Combine remaining ingredients in kettle or heavy saucepan. Cover and simmer 15 minutes.

Okra Chowder (4 to 5 servings)

1 **qt. okra, stems removed and okra sliced**
1½ **cups diced celery**
½ **cup minced green pepper**
1 **medium onion, minced**
¼ **cup butter**
2 **large vine-ripened tomatoes**
1 **tsp. molasses**
½ **tsp. paprika**
4 **cups boiling water**
Sea salt to taste (optional)

Saute' okra, celery, green pepper and onion in butter for 5 minutes. Add tomatoes, molasses, paprika and boiling water. Cover and simmer 45 minutes. Season. Good served with rice.

Onion-Cheddar Chowder (2 to 3 servings)

½ cup chopped onion
2 Tbsp. butter
2 Tbsp. whole wheat flour
Dash vegetable salt (optional)
2 cups raw milk
1 cup shredded natural Cheddar cheese

Saute' onion in butter 5 minutes. Blend in flour and salt. Add milk and bring to boiling, stirring constantly. Remove from heat; add cheese and stir until cheese has melted.

Parsnip Chowder (6 servings)

3 Tbsp. butter
1 medium-sized onion, diced
1½ cups parsnips, diced
1½ cups boiling water
½ tsp. salt
1 tsp. dill weed
4 cups raw milk, scalded

Saute' onion in butter 5 minutes. Add parsnips, potatoes, water, salt and dill; simmer until parsnips and potatoes are tender (approximately 30 minutes). Add milk. Stir to heat. Serve at once.

Potato-Cheese Chowder (serves 4 to 6)

2 cups water
1½ cups diced potatoes
2 vegetable bouillon cubes
2 Tbsp. butter
¼ cup diced green pepper
2 Tbsp. whole wheat flour
1 tsp. vegetable salt (optional)
2 cups raw milk
2 cups grated natural Cheddar cheese

Combine potatoes and water in saucepan. Cover and simmer 15 minutes. Add bouillon and stir to dissolve.

Melt butter in skillet. Saute' green pepper 5 minutes. Stir in flour and salt. Gradually add milk, stirring constantly. Cook until thickened, then stir into potato mixture. Add cheese and stir until smooth. Serve at once.

Potato Chowder (6 servings)

4 large potatoes, scrubbed
2 Tbsp. butter
¼ cup sliced green onions
½ cup chopped green pepper
2 cups Vegetable Stock (page 10)
½ tsp. granulated garlic
½ tsp. paprika
3 Tbsp. whole wheat flour
2 cups raw milk
2 cups cooked dried corn (optional)
½ cup chopped parsley

Dice potatoes. In large saucepan, melt butter. Add onion and green pepper. Cook until tender. Add potatoes, stock and seasoning. Cover and simmer until potatoes are tender. Make paste of flour and ⅓ cup water. Add to potatoe mixture. Add milk and cook until slightly thickened. Stir in corn and parsley. Heat through.

Potato-Corn Chowder (serves 4)

½ cup chopped celery
½ cup chopped green onion
2 Tbsp. butter
2 cups water
2 vegetable bouillon cubes
1½ cups mashed potatoes
1 cup raw corn
1 cup yogurt

Saute' celery and onion in butter. Add water and bouillon. Bring to boiling. Stir in potatoes and corn. Simmer 10 minutes. Stir in yogurt. Serve at once.

Soy-Bean Chowder (5 servings)

2½ cups green soy-beans
2 cups diced potatoes
1½ cups water
½ cup chopped green onions
2 cups fresh corn, pureed
1 cup diced vine-ripened tomatoes
1 Tbsp. safflower oil
½ tsp. vegetable salt (optional)
½ tsp. dried sage
2 cups raw milk, warmed

Cook beans and potatoes in 1½ cups water until vegetables are tender. Add onion, corn, tomatoes, oil, salt and sage. When soup reaches boiling point, remove from heat and stir in milk. Serve at once.

Soya-Macaroni Chowder (4 to 5 servings)

1 Tbsp. safflower oil
¾ cup soya milk
2 Tbsp. grated onion
½ cup green macaroni, cooked
1 cup grated carrot
1½ cups diced raw potatoes
¼ cup minced parsley
4 cups water

In skillet, heat soya milk with oil, stirring constantly until smooth and hot. Add onion, carrots, potatoes, parsley and water. Cover and cook slowly until vegetables are tender-crisp. Add macaroni. Heat and serve.

Tomato Chowder (serves 6)

3 Tbsp. butter
1 medium minced onion
1 cup shredded carrot
1 cup grated potatoes
1 cup diced celery
½ cup boiling water
2 cups ripe tomatoes, diced
4 Tbsp. butter
4 Tbsp. whole wheat flour
¼ tsp. sea salt (optional)
1/8 tsp. cayenne pepper
4 cups raw milk, scalded

Saute' onion, carrot, potatoes and celery in 3 Tbsp. butter until onion is lightly browned. Add water, cover and cook until vegetables are tender. Add tomatoes and heat to boiling.
Melt 4 Tbsp. butter, blend in flour, salt and cayenne. Add milk gradually and cook until smooth. Add vegetable mixture to milk mixture. Heat, but do not boil. Serve at once.

Tomato-Lima Bean Chowder (6 servings)

1 cup water
¼ cup Dry Soup Mix (page 4)
2 cups ripe tomatoes, chopped
2 cups cooked lima beans
2 cups corn cut from cob
½ cup chopped onion
¼ cup minced parsley
2 cloves garlic, crushed
1½ cups raw milk
¼ cup whole wheat flour
¼ tsp. sea salt (optional)
½ tsp. dried thyme
Dash nutmeg (optional)
2 Tbsp. butter

Combine water, soup mix, tomatoes, limas, corn, onion, parsley and garlic in heavy saucepan or kettle. Cover and simmer 15 minutes.
Combine milk, flour, salt, thyme and nutmeg. Mix well. Stir into simmering soup mixture. Stir in butter. Cook 2 minutes.

Wheat Berry Chowder (6 servings)

3 Tbsp. safflower oil
1 Tbsp. whole wheat flour
2 tsp. soy flour
½ cup powdered milk solids
2 cups warm raw milk
2 cups boiling water
½ cup Dry Soup Mix (page 4)
2 cups grated carrot
2 cups cooked whole wheat berries
1 onion, grated

Mix flours and milk powder with oil and blend to form a smooth paste. Add milk and stir until smooth. Blend Dry Soup Mix with boiling water, then stir into milk mixture. Add remaining ingredients. Heat 15 minutes, but do not boil.

Chapter 4

Creamed Soups

Austrian Potato Soup (4 servings)

3 cups Tomato Bouillon (page 9)
½ tsp. cumin seed
1 Tbsp. whole wheat flour
½ cup yogurt
½ cup cream
2 cooked potatoes, cubed

Simmer bouillon with cumin seed for 5 minutes.
Mix flour with yogurt; add small amount of bouillon and beat well. Stir mixture into remaining bouillon. Add cream and potatoes. Heat thoroughly, but do not boil. Serve at once.

Carrot-Cheese Soup (4 to 5 servings)

2 cups raw milk
2 cups Tomato Bouillon (page 9)
1 onion, sliced
4 carrots, diced
½ cup parsley
3 Tbsp. whole wheat flour
¼ cup powdered milk
1 tsp. vegetable salt (optional)
3 Tbsp. butter
½ tsp. dried summer savory
1½ cups natural Cheddar cheese (cubed)

Combine all ingredients. Liquefy in blender container, a little at a time, until all has been liquefied. Heat thoroughly, but do not boil.

Cream of Artichoke Soup (6 servings)

8 large cooked artichoke hearts, mashed
¼ cup butter
3 cups Potato-Vegetable Bouillon (page 8)
2½ cups milk
¼ cup yogurt
Chopped parsley

Heat mashed artichoke hearts in butter in large saucepan a few minutes. Stir in bouillon and milk. Heat to boiling. Stir in yogurt. Garnish with parsley. Serve at once.

Cream of Asparagus Soup (serves 4 to 5)

2 lbs. asparagus, cut into 1" pieces
½ tsp. vegetable salt (optional)
½ cup finely chopped onion
¼ cup butter
2 Tbsp. whole wheat flour
1½ cups Vegetable Stock (page 10)
1 cup yogurt
Dash nutmeg (optional)

Steam asparagus with small amount of water. Add vegetable salt, if desired, and steam until asparagus is tender. Cool slightly, then puree' in blender until smooth.

In large saucepan, saute' onion in butter until onion is tender. Stir in flour; cook over low heat 1 minute. Gradually stir in stock. Bring to boiling, then lower heat and simmer for 3 minutes. Add puree', yogurt and nutmeg. Heat thoroughly. Do not boil.

Cream of Barley Soup (6 servings)

½ cup barley
1 qt. Tomato Bouillon (page 9)
¼ cup chopped celery
¼ cup chopped parsley
½ tsp. dried thyme
½ tsp. vegetable salt (optional)
Dash cayenne
1 cup barley meal
1 qt. raw milk
1 cup yogurt
¼ cup butter

Cook barley in bouillon to which celery, parsley, thyme, salt and cayenne has been added, for 30 minutes. Pour barley meal into simmering soup in continuous stream. Stir in milk and simmer gently 25 minutes. Stir in yogurt and butter. Serve at once.

Cream of Beet Soup (4 servings)

1 medium onion, minced
1 Tbsp. butter
1½ cups water
¼ cup Dry Soup Mix (page 4)
1 cup chopped cooked beets
⅔ cup raw milk
⅓ cup yogurt

Lightly saute' onion in butter. Add water, soup mix and beets. Simmer 15 minutes. Add milk and yogurt. Heat to boiling. Serve at once.

Cream of Broccoli Soup (4 servings)

2 Tbsp. butter
2½ Tbsp. whole wheat flour
1 bunch fresh broccoli
1 medium onion, finely chopped
2 Tbsp. butter
1 qt. Vegetable Stock (page 10)
½ cup yogurt
Vegetable salt to taste (optional)

Melt 2 Tbsp. butter in saucepan. Stir in flour. Cook, stirring, over low heat 3 minutes. Cool.

In large saucepan saute' onion in remaining butter. Chop broccoli into ½" pieces. Stir broccoli into onion-butter mixture. Cover and cook 3 minutes. Stir in broth; heat to simmering. Stir small amount of broth mixture into flour-butter mixture until smooth. Add to saucepan, stirring until smooth. Simmer, covered, 25 minutes.

Remove from heat; cool slightly. Puree with blender or rub through sieve. Return to saucepan. Blend cream into soup. Season to taste.

Cream of Brussels Sprouts Soup (serves 6)

4 cups fresh Brussels sprouts
1 medium onion, chopped
2 cups Vegetable Stock (page 10)
½ tsp. vegetable salt (optional)
Dash cayenne
¼ tsp. thyme
½ tsp. basil
1 cup raw milk

Combine ingredients, except milk, in saucepan. Cover and simmer 20 minutes. Cool slightly, then puree mixture in blender. Return to pan and stir in milk. Heat over low heat, stirring. Do not boil.

Cream of Cabbage Soup (6 servings)

1 green cabbage, shredded
3 medium onions, minced
2 green peppers, chopped
1 ripe tomato, chopped
1 Kitchen Bouquet (page 4)
½ tsp. sea salt (optional)
Dash cayenne
4 cups scalded raw milk
1 cup yogurt
Dash nutmeg
3 Tbsp. butter

Place cabbage, onions and green pepper in kettle; pour in boiling water just to cover vegetables. Add tomatoes, bouquet, salt and cayenne. Cover and simmer until cabbage is tender and water is reduced by half. Blend milk with yogurt and nutmeg; stir into cabbage. Add butter. Cook soup over very low heat until thickened. Serve at once.

Cream of Carrot Soup (4 to 5 servings)

4 carrots, grated
1 medium onion, minced
½ cup minced celery
1½ cups carrot juice
¼ tsp. sea salt (optional)
Dash cayenne
½ cup mashed potato
¾ cup raw milk

Cook carrots, onion and celery in carrot juice in covered saucepan 15 minutes. Add seasoning, potato and milk. Heat, stirring, 5 minutes longer. Do not allow to boil.

Cream of Cauliflower Soup (3 to 4 servings)

2 cups cooked cauliflower
1½ cups water
¼ cup Dry Soup Mix (page 4)
½ Tbsp. curry powder
3 Tbsp. butter
3 Tbsp. whole wheat flour
3 cups raw milk
1 cup yogurt

Cut cauliflower into small pieces and add to water, along with soup mix and curry powder. Heat to boiling; reduce heat and simmer 5 minutes.
Make white sauce using butter, flour and milk. Stir into simmering soup. Heat, but do not boil. Stir in yogurt and serve.

Cream of Celery Soup (serves 10)

2½ cups chopped celery
½ cup butter
½ cup whole wheat flour
2 qts. Potato-Vegetable Bouillon (page 8)
3 celery tops, minced
1 cup yogurt
1 tsp. chervil, minced
Dash nutmeg (optional)
1 Tbsp. grated onion
Minced parsley

Cook celery in butter until tender-crisp. Mix in flour. Gradually stir in 1 qt. bouillon. Add tops. Cover and cook 10 minutes. Put mixture through food mill or puree in blender. Stir in remaining ingredients. Heat slowly. Do not allow to boil.

Cream of Chestnut Soup (3 to 4 servings)

1 lb. boiled chestnuts, peeled and mashed
2 cups raw milk
¼ cup butter
⅔ cup minced onion
1½ Tbsp. whole wheat flour
½ tsp. sea salt (optional)
Dash cloves
Dash cinnamon
½ cup minced celery leaves
1 cup yogurt

Beat together mashed chestnuts and milk. Saute onion in butter. Stir in flour, salt and spices. Slowly add chestnut and milk mixture. Stir in celery leaves. Simmer, stirring 5 minutes. Stir in yogurt. Heat, but do not boil. Serve at once.

Cream of Chicory Soup (5 servings)

1 head tender white chicory, chopped
4 cups Carrot-Turnip Stock (page 5)
1½ cups raw milk
¼ tsp. sea salt (optional)
½ cup yogurt

Steam chicory in small amount of water for 5 minutes. Cool. Puree in blender. Add stock and heat to boiling. Simmer 10 minutes. Stir in milk and salt. Heat to boiling. Remove from heat and stir in yogurt. Serve at once.

Cream of Corn Soup (4 to 5 servings)

2 cups corn cut from cob
3 cups raw milk
2 slices whole wheat bread, crumbled
½ cup diced onion
½ tsp. vegetable salt (optional)
Dash cumin

Combine ingredients in blender container and puree or run through food mill. Pour into saucepan and heat over medium heat 10 minutes, stirring constantly (do not allow to boil).

Cream of Cucumber Soup (3 to 4 servings)

1 large cucumber
4 green onions
½ cup water
½ tsp. sea salt (optional)
1 tsp. dill weed
¾ cup mashed potato
3 sprigs mint, chopped
⅔ cup Vegetable Bouillon (page 9)
⅔ cup yogurt

In blender container or food chopper, finely chop cucumber and onions. Add to saucepan along with water, salt and dill. Simmer, covered 10 minutes. Add remaining ingredients and heat thoroughly. Do not boil.

Cream of Green Bean Soup

3 Tbsp. melted butter
½ cup water
3 cups green beans, snapped into ½" pieces
½ tsp. sea salt (optional)
Dash cayenne
2 cloves garlic, crushed
3 Tbsp. whole wheat flour
1 qt. raw milk
Shredded carrot

In pot, combine butter, water, beans, salt, cayenne and garlic. Cover and simmer 10 minutes.

Blend flour with ¼ cup milk. Stir into simmering soup mixture. Add remaining milk, stirring constantly. Cook until thickened. Garnish with grated carrot.

Cream of Jerusalem Artichoke Soup (6 servings)

3 lbs. Jerusalem artichokes, scrubbed and sliced
2 medium onions, sliced
6 Tbsp. butter
3 cups hot water
½ tsp. sea salt (optional)
3 cups raw milk, heated
1½ cups yogurt
¼ tsp. ground cardamon

Gently saute' artichokes and onions in butter over low heat until tender-crisp. Add hot water and salt. Cook, covered, until vegetables are soft. Cool slightly. Put through food mill. Return to saucepan and add remaining ingredients. Heat thoroughly; do not allow to boil.

Cream of Lettuce Soup (4 servings)

1 lb. leaf lettuce
2 Tbsp. butter
2 Tbsp. grated onion
2 Tbsp. whole wheat flour
3½ cups raw milk
½ tsp. vegetable salt (optional)
½ tsp. dill weed

Cook lettuce in saucepan over medium heat for 6 minutes. Put through food mill or blend to puree.
Melt butter in skillet. Add onion and cook 2 minutes. Stir in flour. Gradually stir in milk. Season with salt and dill. Add cooked lettuce. Heat, but do not boil.

Cream of Lima Soup (4 servings)

½ cup lima bean flour
½ cup powdered onion
1 cup chopped onion
4 cups water
1 tsp. chopped thyme
1 tsp. chopped oregano
½ tsp. vegetable bouillon

Mix flour with powdered milk. Stir in enough water to form a smooth, thin paste. Add remaining water and ingredients. Heat over medium-low heat. Do not allow to boil. Serve at once.

Cream of Mushroom Soup (6 servings)

3 cups minced fresh mushrooms
1 cup minced celery
⅔ cup minced onion
2 Tbsp. butter
2 Tbsp. whole wheat flour
2 cups water
2 cups raw milk
½ cup minced parsley

Saute' mushrooms, celery and onion in butter until softened. Mix flour with small amount of water and stir to form a smooth paste. Stir into 2 cups water. Add to sauteed vegetables. Cook slowly for 20 minutes. Add parsley and cook 10 minutes longer. Stir in milk. Heat thoroughly, but do not boil.

Cream of Onion and Celery Soup (4 servings)

2 medium onions, minced
½ cup minced celery
1½ cups Vegetable Bouillon (page 9)
½ tsp. sea salt (optional)
3 Tbsp. butter
3 Tbsp. whole wheat flour
1½ cups raw milk
Dash ground nutmeg
½ cup yogurt
¼ cup chopped raw cashews

Combine onions, celery, bouillon and salt. Simmer, covered, over medium heat until celery is tender-crisp. Cool slightly. Put in blender container and puree. Heat butter in saucepan. Stir in flour. Gradually add milk, stirring constantly, until mixture is smooth and thickened. Add pureed vegetables and seasoning. Stir in yogurt. Heat thoroughly, stirring constantly. Sprinkle nuts over soup.

Cream of Onion Soup (serves 5)

1 lb. sliced onions
¼ cup butter
3 vegetable bouillon cubes
2 cups boiling water
1 cup cooked brown rice
¼ cup yogurt
2 cups raw milk
3 egg yolks, beaten
½ cup grated natural Swiss cheese

Saute' onions in butter until tender. Dissolve bouillon in boiling water. Add to onions. Cover and simmer 15 minutes. Remove from heat. Puree mixture. Return to pot and add rice. Cook 10 minutes. Stir in yogurt and milk. Blend in yolks. Cook, stirring constantly, until mixture thickens. Remove from heat. Add cheese. Serve immediately.

Cream of Peanut Butter Soup (serves 4 to 5)

¼ cup butter
1 Tbsp. grated onion
1 Tbsp. whole wheat flour
1 cup natural peanut butter
1 qt. Carrot-Spinach Broth (page 5)
Dash nutmeg
¼ tsp. sea salt (optional)
1 cup yogurt

Saute' onion in butter 5 minutes. Add flour and peanut butter. Stir to form a smooth paste. Add broth gradually. Season and simmer 15 minutes, stirring constantly. Add yogurt. Serve at once.

Cream of Potato Soup (4 servings)

4 cups milk
4 medium-sized boiled potatoes, chopped
1 cup chopped onion
½ cup chopped celery
¼ cup chopped celery leaves
¼ cup chopped parsley
½ tsp. vegetable salt (optional)
2 Tbsp. butter

Combine all ingredients. Blend smooth in blender container, 2 cups at a time. Put blended ingredients in saucepan and heat thoroughly (do not boil).

Cream of Pumpkin Soup (4 to 5 servings)

2 Tbsp. butter
2 Tbsp. grated onion
2 Tbsp. whole wheat flour
2 cups mashed cooked pumpkin
2½ cups carrot juice
½ tsp. sea salt (optional)
Dash allspice
½ cup raw milk
½ cup yogurt
1 tsp. grated lemon peel

Saute' onion in butter until soft. Sprinkle flour over sauteed mixture. Stir well. Remove from heat and add pumpkin, carrot juice, salt and allspice. Return to heat and cook, stirring with whisk, until thickened and smooth. Stir in milk, yogurt and lemon rind. Heat, but do not boil. Serve at once.

Cream of Purslane Soup (4 servings)

1½ cups chopped purslane
1 Tbsp. butter
2 Tbsp. freshly squeezed lemon juice
1 tsp. basil
½ tsp. vegetable salt (optional)
2 cups raw milk
2 cups yogurt

Saute' purslane in butter until vegetable has just wilted. Add lemon juice, basil and milk, stirring briskly. Stir in yogurt and heat, but do not boil.

Cream of Sorrel Soup (4 servings)

1 cup sorrel leaves
1 cup spinach leaves
2 Tbsp. butter
4 cups Vegetable Stock (page 10)
Dash nutmeg
1 cup yogurt
3 egg yolks, beaten

Saute' sorrel and spinach in butter 2 to 3 minutes. Add to stock and bring to boiling. Reduce heat and simmer 2 minutes. Remove from heat. Combine nutmeg with yogurt and egg yolks. Mix well. Quickly stir into soup. Heat thoroughly, but do not boil.

Cream of Soy-Bean Soup (4 to 5 servings)

3 cups cooked soybeans, pureed
1 cup raw milk
½ cup yogurt
½ cup powdered milk
1½ cups Vegetable Bouillon (page 9)
1 tsp. chopped chervil

Combine ingredients and mix well. Heat thoroughly, but do not boil. Serve at once.

Cream of Spinach Soup (6 servings)

1 qt. Carrot-Spinach Broth (page 5)
2 lbs. spinach, stemmed
2 Tbsp. wheat germ
1 Tbsp. wheat germ oil
1 onion, chopped
½ tsp. vegetable salt
2 Tbsp. soy flour
⅔ cup milk powder
⅛ tsp. nutmeg
Sesame seeds

Gradually blend all ingredients (except sesame seeds) together in blender. Pour into heavy pot and heat thoroughly (do not boil). Garnish with seeds.

Cream of Squash Soup (serves 5)

2 Tbsp. butter
2 Tbsp. grated onion
2 Tbsp. whole wheat pastry flour
2½ cups pureed cooked winter squash
2½ cups Vegetable Bouillon (page 9)
½ tsp. ground ginger
½ tsp. ground nutmeg
½ tsp. pepper
½ cup cream
1 tsp. grated orange peel

Saute' onion in butter. Sprinkle flour over sauteed onion and stir until bubbly. Remove from heat and add squash, bouillon and seasoning. Return to heat and cook, stirring, until thickened and smooth. Stir in cream and rind. Heat through (do not boil). Serve at once.

Cream of Tomato Soup (4 servings)

2 cups raw milk
2½ cups ripe tomatoes, quartered
2 Tbsp. whole wheat flour
1 Tbsp. honey
½ cup coarsely chopped onion
2 Tbsp. butter
½ tsp. vegetable salt (optional)
1 clove garlic, crushed

Heat milk in saucepan. Put remaining ingredients in blender container and puree. Slowly pour in hot milk and blend a few seconds. Pour into saucepan and reheat over low heat. Serve at once.

Cream of Turnip Soup (serves 4)

2 cups water
2 Tbsp. butter
1 cup carrot juice
1 cup mashed potatoes
2 cups mashed turnips
2 cups raw milk
1 cup yogurt

In kettle, add water, butter, juice, potatoes and turnips. Heat to boiling Add milk and yogurt. Reheat, but do not boil.

Cream of Vegetable Soup (4 servings)

2 cups carrot juice
2 Tbsp. butter
1 Tbsp. flour
½ tsp. vegetable salt (optional)
Dash cayenne
½ cup fresh tomato juice
½ cup cooked carrots
½ cup cooked cauliflower
½ cup fresh raw spinach
2 cups yogurt

Place all ingredients in blender container and blend until smooth. Pour into saucepan and heat over low heat, stirring. So not allow to boil.

Cream of Watercress Soup (serves 4)

3 Tbsp. butter
3 Tbsp. whole wheat flour
3 cups milk
½ tsp. vegetable salt (optional)
Dash cayenne
1½ cup chopped watercress
1 cup boiling water
½ cup yogurt

Melt butter in heavy saucepan. Add flour and stir until smooth. Slowly add milk, stirring. Heat until thickened. Season.
Cook watercress in boiling water 7 minutes. Add to milk sauce. Stir in yogurt. Heat thoroughly, but do not boil.

Cream of Zucchini Soup (4 to 6 servings)

1 cup thinly sliced onion
2½ Tbsp. safflower oil
3 cups grated zucchini
¼ tsp. dill weed
5 cups Vegetable Stock (page 10)
1 cup ricotta cheese
1 cup raw milk
Grated natural Swiss cheese

Saute' onion in oil. Stir in zucchini and dill and continue cooking for 4 to 5 minutes. Add stock and simmer, covered, for 15 minutes. Cool slightly, then slowly and ricotta cheese. Stir in milk. Heat, but do not boil. Sprinkle with grated cheese and serve at once.

Curried Watercress Soup (4 to 5 servings)

½ cup butter
½ cup whole wheat flour
¼ tsp. vegetable salt (optional)
¾ tsp. curry powder
3½ cups raw milk
1½ cups shredded carrot
½ cup boiling water
1 cup chopped watercress
1 Tbsp. grated coconut

Melt butter in saucepan; blend in flour, salt and curry powder. Gradually stir in milk and cook, stirring constantly, until smooth and thickened. Set aside. Cook carrots with boiling water for 3 minutes. Add carrots, cooking liquid and watercress to hot milk mixture. Stir well. Heat thoroughly, but do not boil. Sprinkle with coconut and serve at once.

Hot Cream of Avocado Soup (5 to 6 servings)

2 medium avocado, peeled and mashed
3 cups raw milk
2 cups yogurt
¼ tsp. celery seed
1 clove garlic, crushed
Dash cayenne

Combine all ingredients. Mix well. Pour into saucepan and heat. Do not boil. Serve at once.

Sour Cream Potato Soup (serves 6)

2 cups diced potatoes
1 cup boiling water
½ tsp. vegetable salt (optional)
1 medium onion, diced
⅛ tsp. cayenne
2 cups sour cream
Minced parsley

Combine potatoes, water, salt, onion and cayenne. Simmer, covered, 25 minutes. Add cream and cook 5 minutes longer. Garnish with parsley.

Swiss Cream of Potato Soup (serves 6 to 8)

4 medium potatoes, cooked and mashed
½ cup minced onion
2 Tbsp. butter
2 Tbsp. minced parsley
1 tsp. vegetable salt (optional)
¼ tsp. nutmeg
⅛ tsp. cayenne
¼ tsp. dry mustard
2 tsp. Tamari soy sauce
3 cups raw milk
1 cup grated natural *Swiss cheese*

Saute' onion in butter until tender. Add onion, along with parsley, salt, nutmeg, cayenne, mustard and soy sauce to mashed potatoes. Mix well. Stir in milk. Heat thoroughly, stirring constantly (do not allow to boil). Sprinkle with cheese and serve at once.

Chapter 5

Fruit Soup

Apple Bouillon (4 to 5 servings)

>1 lb. apples, cored and diced
>2½ pints Clear Mushroom Stock (page 6)
>2 cloves
>2 crushed whole cardamons
>⅛ tsp. grated ginger root
>Yogurt

Combine apples, stock, cloves, cardamons and ginger in large saucepan. Cover and simmer 20 minutes. Remove cloves. Press through sieve or puree in blender. Reheat. Garnish each serving with a spoonful of yogurt (providing those served like yogurt).

Autumn Pear Soup (6 servings)

>1½ Tbsp. butter
>1 cup minced onion
>3 ripe pears, diced
>1 Tbsp. curry powder
>3 cups Vegetable Stock (page 10)
>1½ cups cottage cheese
>½ cup raw milk
>½ cup slivered almonds

Saute' onion in butter for 5 minutes. Add pears and stir. Sprinkle with curry and cook 1 minute. Add stock; cover and simmer 10 minutes. Cool.

Blend together cottage cheese and milk. Stir into chilled soup. Refrigerate until serving time. Garnish with nuts.

Banana-Coconut Soup (serves 4)

1 Tbsp. butter
1 cup minced onion
1½ cups freshly squeezed orange juice
½ cup unsweetened shredded coconut
3 bananas, cut-up
2 cups milk
1 cup yogurt

Saute' onion in butter 5 minutes. Put in blender container, along with orange juice, coconut and bananas. Puree. Pour into bowl. Stir in milk and yogurt. Chill.

Bing Cherry Soup (4 servings)

1 lb. bing cherries, stoned
1 stick cinnamon
2 tsp. grated lemon peel
1 cup hot water
1 cup cherry juice
1 Tbsp. honey
1 cup unsweetened pineapple juice
½ Tbsp. cornstarch
Yogurt

Combine all ingredients (except yogurt) and mix well. Bring to boiling and cook 10 minutes. Puree through food sieve or food mill. Heat. Serve topped with a spoonful of yogurt.

Chilled Apple Soup (5 to 6 servings)

4 cored, diced apples
¼ cup honey
1 Tbsp. grated lemon rind
3 cups hot water
2 Tbsp. cider vinegar
2 Tbsp. whole wheat flour
2 Tbsp. cold water
½ cup yogurt
Dash cinnamon

Combine apples, honey, rind and hot water. Cook until apples are tender.
Blend flour with cold water. Add vinegar. Stir into apple mixture. Cook 5 minutes. Chill. Stir in yogurt. Garnish with a sprinkle of cinnamon.

Chilled Raspberry Soup (3 to 4 servings)

½ cup water
4 cups fresh raspberries
1 tsp. freshly squeezed lemon juice
Yogurt

Combine water, raspberries and lemon juice in blender container and puree. Strain through several layers of cheese cloth. Chill. Serve topped with a spoonful of yogurt.

Chilled Strawberry-Rhubarb Soup (6 servings)

1 lb. fresh rhubarb, cut-up
½ cup water
⅓ cup honey
1 cup unsweetened pineapple juice
2 cups fresh strawberries, mashed
1 Tbsp. freshly squeezed lemon juice
Dash nutmeg

Cook rhubarb with water and honey 10 minutes. Cool. Add remaining ingredients to rhubarb. Put through food mill or puree in blender. Chill.

Citrus-Yogurt Soup (serves 4)

3 Tbsp. honey
1 cup water
2 Tbsp. grated orange rind
2 tsp. grated lemon rind
1 cup freshly squeezed orange juice
½ cup freshly squeezed lemon juice
1 cup yogurt

Combine honey and water. Boil 5 minutes. Remove from heat and add rind. Cool. Add juice and yogurt. Chill.

Curried Fruit Soup (4 servings)

1 Tbsp. butter
1 medium onion, diced
1 medium apple, cored and diced
1 medium pear, cored and diced
1 semi-ripe banana, peeled and diced
½ cup raisins
2 cups Bran Broth (page 5)
1 Tbsp. curry powder
1 cup yogurt
Grated coconut

Melt butter in large skillet. Add onion, fruits and raisins. Stir-fry 4 to 5 minutes. Add broth and curry. Cover and simmer 20 minutes, stirring occasionally. Puree in blender or food mill. Chill. At serving time, stir in yogurt. Garnish with grated coconut.

Curry-Coconut Soup (4 to 5 servings)

4 Tbsp. butter
1½ cups grated coconut
2 Tbsp. whole wheat flour
3 cups Vegetable Bouillon (page 9)
1 Tbsp. curry powder
½ cup raisins
½ cup yogurt
½ cup roasted peanuts

Brown coconut in butter. Sprinkle flour over; stir to blend. Slowly add bouillon, stirring constantly. Add curry and raisin. Cover and simmer 12 minutes. Remove from heat. Stir in yogurt. Garnish with peanuts just before serving.

Dried Fruit-Elderberry Soup

2 Tbsp. arrowroot starch
2 cups water
1½ cups dried mixed fruit
1 cup dried elderberries
3 cups water
¼ cup honey

Soak dried fruit and berries in 3 cups water overnight.
Blend arrowroot into 2 cups water. Stir into fruit and soaking liquid. Heat to boiling. Cover and simmer 25 minutes. Add honey and cook 5 minutes longer.

Dried Fruit Soup (6 to 8 servings)

1½ cups dried apricots
1 cup pitted dried prunes
6 cups freshly squeezed orange juice
1 tsp. grated lemon rind
1 Tbsp. freshly squeezed lemon juice
1-3" piece cinnamon stick
1 Tbsp. arrowroot
¼ cup honey
½ cup yogurt
¼ cup grated orange rind

Combine dried fruit, orange juice, lemon juice, lemon rind and cinnamon. Let stand 30 minutes, then simmer, covered 10 minutes. Add arrowroot and honey. Simmer until slightly thickened. Cool. Serve with a dab of yogurt and grated orange rind.

Fresh Apricot-Raspberry Soup (6 servings)

2½ cups diced apricots
1 cup raspberries
2 Tbsp. honey
1 cup cottage cheese
2 cups yogurt
½ cup raw milk
1 tsp. grated orange peel

Puree ingredients in blender. Chill well before serving.

Fresh Prune Soup (serves 5)

1 lb. fresh ripe prunes, pitted
3 cups water
1 Tbsp. arrowroot starch
¼ cup freshly squeezed lemon juice
⅓ cup honey
1½ cups yogurt

Place prunes and water in kettle. Cover and simmer 20 minutes. Cool slightly, then puree in blender.
Combine starch with lemon juice and stir until smooth. Slowly stir into puree. Heat to boiling. Stir in honey and cook 5 minutes. Serve at once topped with yogurt.

Fresh Rose Hip Soup (serves 4)

2 cups rose hips, halved and seeded
4 cups water
¼ cup honey
1 Tbsp. arrowroot starch
1½ cups water

Simmer rose hips in 4 cups water for 30 minutes. Cool. Puree in blender. Add arrowroot to 1½ cups water and blend well. Add to puree along with honey. Simmer 5 minutes. Serve hot.

Green Grape Soup (4 servings)

1 quart seedless grapes, removed from stems
2 Tbsp. honey
1 quart water
1-1" piece cinnamon stick

Combine all ingredients in saucepan. Cover and simmer 15 minutes. Serve hot or chilled.

Melon Soup (serves 12)

2 cups halved strawberries
4 cantaloupes, rind and seeds removed
4 cups freshly squeezed orange juice
⅔ cups freshly squeezed lime juice
2 cups papaya juice
2 cups water
Mint sprigs

Cube cantaloupes. Place strawberries and cantaloupe pieces in blender container and puree. Stir in fruit juices and water. Chill. Stir before serving. Garnish with mint.

Orange Bouillon (4 servings)

1 Tbsp. unflavored gelatin
1½ cups freshly squeezed orange juice
¼ cup honey
1 Tbsp. freshly squeezed lemon juice
3 oranges, peeled sectioned and diced

Combine gelatin with ½ cup orange juice and allow to soften 5 minutes. Heat remaining orange juice; add gelatin mixture and stir until dissolved. Stir in honey and lemon juice. Chill.
When mixture starts to set, beat with whisk. Repeat chilling and beating process several times. Add diced oranges and chill again. Beat well before serving.

Orange Soup (3 servings)

3 cups freshly squeezed orange juice
1 Tbsp. cornstarch
⅓ cup water
1 Tbsp. honey

Heat fruit juice in saucepan. Mix cornstarch with water and stir into soup. Cook slowly, stirring until thickened. Add honey. Chill. (Nice served in chilled wine glasses.)

Peach Soup (6 servings)

3½ cups diced peaches
2 Tbsp. honey
1½ cups yogurt
2 cups buttermilk
1 tsp. grated orange peel
¼ cup freshly squeezed orange juice

Combine all ingredients in blender container. Puree until smooth. Chill.

Pineapple Soup (4 servings)

4 cups fresh pineapple juice
2½ Tbsp. cornstarch
½ cup water
1 Tbsp. honey

Heat juice in saucepan. Mix cornstarch with water and stir into hot soup. Cook over low heat, stirring, until clear. Chill. Serve in chilled bowls or dessert cups.

Rose Hip-Prune Soup (6 servings)

3 cups fresh rose hips, seeds removed
2 qts. boiling water
2 Tbsp. pinyon nuts
⅓ cup pure maple syrup
18 cooked, pitted prunes

Cook rose hips in 2 quarts boiling water until tender. Strain through sieve; discard solids. Add nuts and syrup. Bring to boiling, stirring constantly. Allow to cool. Chill. To serve, place 3 prunes in each serving bowl. Ladle rose hip soup over prunes.

Strawberry-Pineapple Soup (4 servings)

2 cups strawberry juice
1½ cups pineapple juice
1 cup stewed bing cherries
2 Tbsp. freshly squeezed lemon juice
2 Tbsp. arrowroot starch
1 cup strong chilled rose hip tea

Stir arrowroot into tea, heat over medium heat until blended. Add remaining ingredients and heat slightly. Serve warm or chilled.

Chapter 6

Main Course Soups

Autumn Minestrone (6 servings)

1½ cups dried white beans, soaked overnight and drained
1 medium head cabbage, shredded
1 medium onion, minced
1 leek, sliced
1 carrot, grated
½ cup celery (chopped)
¼ cup minced parsley
5 potatoes, thinly sliced
2 turnips, thinly sliced
1 tsp. sea salt (optional)
2 qts. Clear Mushroom Stock (page 6)
¾ cup broken whole wheat spaghetti noodles
2 Tbsp. butter
1 cup grated Parmesan cheese

Cook beans in salted water to cover for 1½ hours or until tender; drain and set aside.

Add onion, leek, carrot, celery, parsley, potatoes, turnips, salt and mushroom stock. Simmer ½ hour. Add spaghetti and beans and simmer 10 to 12 minutes longer. Add butter and cheese. Serve at once.

Barley-Mushroom Soup (6 servings)

½ cup chopped onion
1 leek, chopped
3 Tbsp. butter
1 cup grated carrots
½ cup barley
½ tsp. sea salt (optional)
4 peppercorns, crushed
2 qts. water
2 cups diced unpeeled potatoes
2 bay leaves
1 lb. mushrooms, sliced
1 cup yogurt

Saute' onion and leek in butter until tender. Add carrots, barley, salt, peppercorns and 2 qts. water. Bring to boiling. Lower heat and simmer until barley is tender. Add potatoes, bay leaves and mushrooms. Simmer 30 minutes. Remove bay. Mix in yogurt just before serving.

Barley-Vegetable Soup (6 to 8 servings)

2 qts. water
⅔ cup barley
¼ cup buckwheat groats
2 bay leaves
1 cup diced celery
2½ cups grated potatoes
1 cup grated carrots
½ cup minced onion
1 cup chopped ripe tomatoes
1 cup fresh or dried and cooked lima beans
1 cup chopped broccoli
2 Tbsp. minced parsley
1½ cups chopped zucchini

In kettle, combine water, barley, groats and bay. Cook over medium heat until barley and groats are soft. Add remaining ingredients and cook 15 minutes over medium heat. Season to taste. Remove bay before serving.

Bean Porridge (serves 6)

1 pint black beans
2 Tbsp. grated onion
2 stalks celery, chopped
1 tsp. vegetable salt (optional)
2 cloves
2 qts. Potato Vegetable Bouillon (page 8)
1 hard-cooked egg yolk, riced
½ tsp. dry mustard
1 Tbsp. butter

Cover beans with water and soak overnight. Drain and rinse. Put in kettle along with onion, celery, salt, cloves and bouillon. Simmer until beans are soft. Puree in blender or rub through a sieve. Add yolk, pepper, mustard and butter. Stir well. Heat to boiling.

Black Bean Soup (serves 6)

1½ cups cooked brown rice
⅓ cup minced onion
3 Tbsp. olive oil
3 Tbsp. cider vinegar
¼ cup butter
2 medium onions, minced
2 green peppers, chopped
8 large cloves garlic, pressed
3 cups water
4 vegetable bouillon cubes
2 tsp. ground cumin
1½ tsp. dried oregano leaves
2 Tbsp. cider vinegar
6 cups cooked black turtle beans

Combine ⅓ cup minced onion, olive oil and 3 Tbsp. vinegar with rice. Set aside.
Melt butter in Dutch oven or kettle. Add onion, green pepper and garlic. Saute' 5 minutes. Add water, bouillon, seasonings, vinegar and beans. Cover and simmer for 30 minutes. Serve in bowls topped with marinated rice

Black Soybean Soup (serves 6 to 8)

2 cups black soybeans
⅓ cup diced celery
2 qts. water
¼ cup Dry Soup Mix (page 4)
2 Tbsp. butter
2 Tbsp. whole wheat flour
½ tsp. vegetable salt (optional)
Dash cayenne
¼ tsp. dry mustard
2 hard-cooked eggs, sliced
1 lemon, in thin slices

Soak beans overnight; drain. Add celery, water and soup mix. Simmer in covered pot or kettle 4 hours. Pour mixture in food mill or blender and puree.
Melt butter in skillet; stir in flour, seasoning and bean puree. Reheat. Pour over eggs and lemon slices. Serve at once.

Broccoli-Cheese Soup (serves 4)

2 cups raw milk
3 Tbsp. melted butter
3 Tbsp. grated onion
3 Tbsp. whole wheat flour
Dash cayenne
2 cups shredded natural Cheddar cheese
1 Tbsp. minced fresh thyme
2 cloves garlic, crushed
2 vegetable bouillon cubes
2 cups boiling water
2 cups cooked, chopped broccoli

Saute' onion in butter. Blend in flour and pepper. Add milk, stirring constantly. Cook and stir until mixture thickens. Add cheese, stir until melted, then remove form heat.
Dissolve bouillon in water. Stir into cheese mixture. Stir in broccoli. Heat, but do not boil.

Brown Rice-Fresh Pea Soup (serves 3 to 4)

3 cups Rich Vegetable Stock (page 8)
2 Tbsp. whole wheat flour
½ tsp. vegetable salt (optional)
¼ cup milk powder
½ cup raw brown rice
3 Sprigs fresh dill, chopped
1 tsp. fresh basil
½ cup raw milk
2 cups fresh raw peas
1 Tbsp. freshly squeezed lemon juice

In top of double boiler over direct heat, bring stock to boiling. Mix flour, salt and milk powder together. Stir into boiling stock. Add rice. Place top of double boiler over bottom to which hot water has been added. Simmer, covered, 45 minutes. Add remaining ingredients. Heat thoroughly and serve.

Cheddar Cheese Soup (serves 4 to 5)

3 cups milk
2 Tbsp. butter
1 clove garlic, crushed
2 Tbsp. whole wheat flour
½ lb. natural Cheddar cheese, grated
⅛ tsp. cayenne
⅛ tsp. nutmeg (optional)
1 cup carrot juice
2 egg yolks
½ cup yogurt

Heat milk in saucepan. Melt butter in skillet. Add garlic and saute' a few minutes. Stir in flour. Add small amount of heated milk, stir smooth, then stir mixture into remaining heated milk. Add cheese, cayenne and nutmeg and heat, stirring until cheese melts (do not allow mixture to boil). Add carrot juice. Mix well.

Beat together egg yolks and yogurt. Add ½ cup of soup mixture to yolk mixture and stir briskly. Add yolk-soup mixture to bulk of soup and mix well. Heat a few minutes longer. Serve at once.

Chick Pea-Pasta Soup (8 servings)

2 cups dried chick peas, soaked overnight and drained
3 qts. cold water
½ tsp. dried rosemary
3 cloves garlic, crushed
1 tsp. vegetable salt
Dash cayenne
½ lb. vegetable macaroni

Put chick peas, water, rosemary, garlic, salt and cayenne in pot. Bring to a boil. Reduce heat and simmer 1½ hours. Add macaroni and cook 10 to 12 minutes.

Cornmeal Soup (4 servings)

¼ cup cornmeal
1½ cups raw milk
2 cups carrot juice
2 cups Onion-Garlic Broth (page 7)
1 cup grated natural Cheddar cheese

Combine cornmeal and milk in top of double boiler over simmering water; heat and stir until thick mush is formed. Stir in juice, broth and cheese. Continue to heat and stir until cheese melts.

Corn Tortilla Soup (4 servings)

6 corn tortillas
¼ cup corn oil
½ onion, chopped
2 cloves garlic, crushed
½ tsp. coriander
⅛ cup minced fresh mint
1 cup grated natural Cheddar cheese
1 cup fresh tomato puree
2 qts. Vegetable Soup Base (page 10)
Guacamole

Slice tortillas into strips 1" wide and 2" long. Heat oil in skillet; add tortilla strips and fry crisp. Remove from pan; drain. Add onion, garlic, coriander and mint to oil in which tortillas were fried. Cook until onion is tender. Add tomato puree and cook 3 minutes. Add to tortilla strips and cheese in kettle. Add soup base and heat. Top with guacamole, if desired.

Cracked Corn Minestrone (serves 6)

1 cup cracked corn
½ cup uncooked brown rice
2 quarts Vegetable Stock (page 10)
½ cup minced onion
½ cup butter, melted
1 cup shredded cabbage
1 diced leek
1 cup grated carrot
1 cup diced zucchini
2 cloves garlic, crushed
½ cup fresh peas
1 cup diced ripe tomatoes
¼ tsp. vegetable salt (optional)

Cover corn with water and allow to soak overnight. Cook soaked corn in liquid for 2 hours. Drain.
Put stock in kettle. Add rice and onion. Simmer 30 minutes. Saute' cabbage, leek, carrot, zucchini and garlic in butter. Add to stock and simmer 10 minutes. Add peas, tomatoes, corn and salt. Simmer 10 to 15 minutes longer.

Dutch Bean Soup (serves 6)

1 cup navy beans
2 quarts water
1 quart carrot juice
½ tsp. sea salt (optional)
1 onion, grated
1 cup yogurt

Soak beans overnight in water to cover. Drain. Cook beans in 2 quarts water plus carrot juice until beans have reach the consistency of rich cream. Add salt and onion. Heat to boiling. Stir in yogurt. Serve at once.

Dutch Vegetable Soup (serves 8)

2 cups dried lima beans
Water
½ cup Dry Soup Mix (page 4)
2 cups chopped ripe tomatoes
2 cups grated fresh corn
2 cups shredded cabbage
1 large turnip, diced
2 carrots, grated
1 onion, diced
1 tsp. whole wheat flour
½ cup raw milk
Grated natural Cheddar cheese

Soak beans in water, to cover, overnight. Add 1 quart water, soup mix and vegetables. Cover and simmer 45 minutes. Mix flour with milk and stir into simmering soup. Cook 10 minutes longer. Serve in warmed bowls. Garnish with grated cheese.

Egg-Bread Casserole Soup (serves 6)

>   6 slices whole wheat bread
>   6 Tbsp. butter
>   12 eggs
>   6 Tbsp. fresh tomato puree
>   6 vegetable bouillon cubes
>   6 cups boiling water
>   1 cup grated natural Cheddar cheese
>   1 tsp. fresh chopped oregano

Butter bread. Place a slice in each of 6 individual oven-proof bowls. Bake at 400°F. until butter melts and edges of bread browns. Remove from heat. Break 2 eggs over bread in each bowl. Top each with 1 Tbsp. tomato puree.

Dissolve bouillon in boiling water. Add 1 cup bouillon to each bowl. Sprinkle grated cheese over each, return to oven and bake 10 minutes or until cheese melts and egg whites set. Garnish with oregano.

Egg Soup (serves 4)

>   1 chopped onion
>   2 Tbsp. butter
>   2 Tbsp. flour
>   1 tsp. sea salt (optional)
>   1 cup hot tomato juice
>   2 cups boiling water
>   1 bay leaf
>   1 Tbsp. freshly squeezed lemon juice
>   ½ cup yogurt
>   8 poached eggs

Saute' onion in butter for 5 minutes. Blend in flour, salt and tomato juice. Stir until thickened and smooth. Add water, bay and lemon juice. Boil 1 minutes. Remove from heat. Discard bay. Stir in yogurt. Serve over poached eggs.

Garden Fresh Vegetable Soup (serves 6)

3 Tbsp. butter
2 cups chopped onion
2 cloves garlic, pressed
1 cup shredded carrots
1½ cups diced potatoes
1 cup fresh raw corn kernels
1½ cups diced zucchini
1 cup fresh peas
2 quarts Vegetable Stock (page 10)
2 cups cooked kidney beans
1 tsp. dried basil
½ tsp. dried oregano
½ tsp. rosemary
1 cup pureed fresh ripe tomato
2 cups chopped ripe tomato
⅔ cup whole wheat macaroni
2 cups shredded spinach

Saute' onion and garlic in butter in large kettle for 5 minutes. Add carrots, potatoes, corn, stock and herbs. Simmer, covered 30 minutes. Add pureed tomato, diced tomatoes and macaroni. Cook, covered, 20 minutes. Add zucchini, peas and spinach. Cover and simmer 7 minutes longer.

Lentil and Chard Soup (6 servings)

2 cups lentils
2½ lbs. *Swiss chard, chopped*
2 cups water
½ cup olive oil
1 cup chopped onion
4 cloves garlic, crushed
½ cup chopped celery
½ tsp. *vegetable salt* (optional)
1 cup freshly squeezed lemon juice
1 tsp. whole wheat flour

Cover lentiles with cold water and cook, covered, until tender. Add chard and water to lentils and cook until chard is done.
Saute' onion, garlic and celery in olive oil until vegetable are tender. Stir vegetables into lentil mixture. Mix lemon juice with salt and flour. Stir into lentil-vegetable mixture. Cook gently, stirring frequently, until soup has thickened.

Lentil-Curry Soup (3 to 4 servings)

½ cup lentils
6 cups water
¼ cup chopped onion
2 cloves minced garlic
1 Tbsp. butter
¼ tsp. chili powder
3 tsp. curry powder
2 tsp. lemon juice
Sea salt (optional)

Cook lentils in water for 1 hour. Saute' onion and garlic in butter with chili and curry powder. Add mixture to lentil soup, along with lemon juice and salt. Simmer 10 minutes longer.

Mexican Avocado Soup (serves 6)

2 Tbsp. olive oil
1 large onion, chopped
2 cloves garlic, minced
1½ quarts Vegetable Bouillon (page 9)
3 ripe tomatoes, chopped
2 carrots, thinly sliced
2 potatoes, scrubbed and diced
1 tsp. honey
1 tsp. vegetable salt (optional)
½ tsp. pepper
2 medium avocado
Lemon juice
2 cups grated natural Monterey Jack cheese
2 cups grated natural Cheddar cheese
    Condiments:
Yogurt
Chopped green onions
Hard-cooked eggs, chopped
Tortilla chips

   Saute' onion and garlic in olive oil. Add bouillon, tomatoes, carrots, potatoes, honey, salt and pepper. Bring to boiling, then reduce heat, cover and simmer 25 minutes. Line soup bowls with grated cheese and avocado slices which have been dipped in lemon juice. Ladle hot soup into bowls, then pass the condiments.

Mozzarella Cheese Soup (serves 4)

4 onions, sliced
½ cup butter
1 Tbsp. arrowroot
½ cup water
2 vegetable bouillon cubes
2 cups boiling water
3 cups raw milk
2 egg yolks, beaten
⅔ cup grated natural Mozzarella cheese
1 Tbsp. chopped parsley
1 cup whole wheat croutons

Saute' onion in butter for 5 minutes.
Dissolve arrowroot in ½ cup water. Add to onions along with bouillon cubes boiling water and milk. Cook slowly, stirring often, until heated.
Blend together egg yolks, cheese and 1 cup soup. Add to pot. Heat, but do not boil. Garnish with parsley and croutons.

Meatless Minestrone (6 to 8 servings)

2 cups diced onion
3 carrots, diced
3 stalks celery, sliced
2 medium potatoes, diced
2½ quarts Mushroom Bouillon (page 7)
2 medium-sized zucchini, sliced
3 ripe tomatoes, chopped
1 cup long grain rice
1 tsp. sea salt (optional)
3 cloves garlic, crushed
1½ tsp. thyme
1 cup uncooked whole wheat macaroni
2 cups cooked garbanzo beans
Whole wheat croutons

Put first 11 ingredients in large soup kettle and bring to boiling. Reduce heat and simmer 2½ to 3 hours. Add macaroni and garbanzo beans. Cover and simmer until macaroni is cooked. Serve with croutons.

Mushroom-Barley Soup

½ lb. fresh mushrooms, sliced
3 Tbsp. butter
1 onion, chopped
5 cups Clear Mushroom Stock (page 6)
¼ cup barley
1 clove garlic, crushed
2 bay leaves
¼ cup minced parsley
Dash cayenne
2 Tbsp. whole wheat flour
1½ cups raw milk
Grated natural Swiss cheese

Saute' onion in butter. Add mushrooms, stock, barley, garlic, bay, parsley and cayenne. Cover and simmer 45 minutes. Discard bay.
Mix flour with milk until smooth. Stir into soup. Cook, stirring, until heated. Garnish with cheese.

Mushroom Noodle Soup (serves 4 to 5)

1 lb. chopped mushrooms
3 Tbsp. melted butter
2 Tbsp. minced onion
2 Tbsp. whole wheat flour
6 vegetable bouillon cubes
6 cups boiling water
⅛ tsp. cayenne
1 clove garlic, crushed
1 cup Green Noodles (page 121)
¾ cup yogurt
Paparika

Saute' mushrooms and onion in butter for 5 minutes. Stir in flour. Add bouillon cubes and water. Bring to boiling. Add cayenne, garlic and noodles. Cover and simmer 15 minutes. Stir in yogurt. Garnish with paparika and serve at once.

Mushroom Soup with Tofu (serves 6)

    8 cups vegetable bouillon
    1 Tbsp. Tamari soy sauce
    1 lb. sliced mushrooms
    1 Tbsp. chopped green onion
    1 lb. tofu, cut into squares
    Chopped green onion

    Combine bouillon with Tamari in 3 quart pot. Bring to boiling; add mushrooms, 1 Tbsp. green onion and tofu; simmer gently 25 minutes. Garnish with green onions.

Pinÿon Nut Soup (6 servings)

    1 cup Mushroom Broth (page 7)
    1 cup whole milk
    2 cups shelled pinÿon nuts
    2 medium onions, chopped
    2 Tbsp. peanut oil
    1/8 tsp. powdered cloves
    1/4 tsp. powdered allspice
    1 tsp. sea salt (optional)
    Yogurt

    In blender container, blend together broth, milk, nuts, onion, oil, spices and salt until smooth.
    Heat thoroughly. Serve topped with a spoonful of yogurt.

Quebec Pea Soup (4 to 5 servings)

½ lb. dried split yellow peas
6 cups cold water
½ cup Dry Soup Mix (page 4)
¼ cup grated carrot
½ cup grated onion
½ cup grated turnip
2 cloves garlic, crushed
¼ tsp. dried savory
Sea salt to taste (optional)

Combine peas with water and soup mix. Bring to boiling. Skim; add vegetables, garlic and savory. Simmer, covered 2 hours. Season to taste.

Soybean-Vegetable Soup (6 servings)

1 cup dried soybeans, cooked and mashed
1 cup Vegetable Stock (page 10)
½ cup celery, chopped
1 onion, grated
3 cloves garlic, crushed
½ cup chopped green pepper
1 cup raw milk
1 Tbsp. whole wheat flour
1 tsp. sea salt (optional)
1 tsp. thyme
1 cup ripe tomatoes, chopped
½ cup grated turnip
½ cup grated carrot
½ cup sunflower seeds

Combine all ingredients in kettle. Cover with tight fitting lid and simmer 20 minutes.

Split Pea Soup (6 servings)

1 cup dried split green peas
3 quarts water
2 bay leaves
2 large potatoes, grated
5 green onions, sliced
3 stalks celery, chopped
3 cloves garlic, crushed
1 tsp. vegetable salt (optional)
¼ tsp. ground cinnamon
Dash cloves

Soak peas overnight; drain. Add water and bay; bring to boiling. Skin foam. Add remaining ingredients and simmer 2 hours. Remove bay. Puree soup in blender or food mill if you wish a smooth soup.

Springtime Minestrone (6 servings)

1 cup fresh basil leaves
1 cup spinach leaves
¼ cup grated Parmesan
2 Tbsp. minced parsley
4 cloves garlic, minced
3 Tbsp. oil
¼ lb. spinach, torn
¼ lb. beet greens, torn
¼ lb. cooked lima beans
½ head cabbage, shredded
3 small potatoes, grated
1 medium onion, minced
1 bunch green onions, sliced
1 tsp. vegetable salt (optional)
2 quarts water
½ lb. uncooked whole wheat macaroni

Whirl basil, 1 cup spinach, Parmesan, garlic and parsley in blender at high speed for 30 seconds.
Heat oil in kettle. Add spinach, greens, limas, cabbage, potatoes, green onions and salt. Cook 2 minutes. Add water, cover and simmer 1½ hours. Add macaroni and cook until tender. With wire whisk, add blended ingredients to soup. Heat and serve.

Vegetable-Cheese Soup (6 servings)

3 Tbsp. butter
1 cup chopped celery
1 cup shredded carrot
½ cup chopped onion
3 vegetable bouillon cubes
4 cups water
⅛ tsp. cayenne
1½ cups mashed potatoes
2 cups raw milk
2 cups shredded natural Cheddar cheese

Saute' celery, carrot and onion in butter 8 minutes. Add bouillon, water and cayenne. Cover and simmer 20 minutes. Stir in potatoes, milk and cheese. Heat until cheese has melted. Do not boil. Serve at once.

Vegetable-Rice Soup (4 servings)

2 potatoes, diced
2 medium turnips, diced
1 cup cooked kidney beans
½ cup chopped cabbage
½ cup diced celery
1 quart Mushroom Broth (page 7)
½ cup uncooked brown rice
Sea salt (optional)
Pinch saffron (optional)

Cook vegetables and rice in stock until vegetables are tender and rice is cooks. Season with salt and saffron.

Wheat Bread Soup (serves 4 to 5)

1 quart Tomato Bouillon (page 9)
7 slices whole grain bread
2 eggs, beaten
1 cup yogurt
3 Tbsp. butter

Crumble bread into bouillon and bring to boiling. Reduce heat and simmer 10 minutes.

Beat together eggs and yogurt. Remove soup from heat and vigorously beat egg mixture into soup. Add butter and beat until butter has melted. Serve at once.

White Kidney Bean-Basil Soup (6 to 8 servings)

½ lb. dried white kidney beans
5 cloves
2 bay leaves
1 lb. turnips, diced
2 medium-sized potatoes, diced
1 lb. carrots, diced
3 small onions, chopped
1 lb. ripe tomatoes chopped
3 Tbsp. fresh basil
⅛ tsp. cayenne
1 lb. zucchini, diced
2 tsp. vegetable salt (optional)
2 Tbsp. olive oil
¼ cup minced parsley

Soak beans overnight in water to cover. Drain beans and rinse in cold water. Put in heavy kettle. Add 6 cups water to drained beans. Bring to boiling over medium heat. Add cloves and bay. Cover and simmer 2 hours. Add potatoes, onions, carrots, turnips, basil and cayenne. Simmer, covered, 20 minutes. Add remaining ingredients and simmer, covered, 10 minutes longer.

Chapter 7

Vegetable Soups

Acorn Squash Soup (serves 5 to 6)

3 cups cooked, mashed acorn squash
½ cup minced onion
½ cup minced celery
2 Tbsp. butter
4 cups Onion-Garlic Broth (page 7)
1 tsp. molasses
½ tsp. cinnamon
¼ tsp. nutmeg
¼ tsp. cloves
1 cup yogurt
½ cup broken raw cashews

Saute' onion and celery in butter for 5 minutes. Add squash, broth, molasses and spices. Heat to boiling. Stir in yogurt. Serve at once. Garnish with cashews.

Alpine Soup (serves 4)

1 cup chopped onions
3 Tbsp. butter
1 cup diced ripe tomatoes
3½ cups Vegetable Stock (page 10)
1½ tsp. dried oregano
1 cup sprouted wheat
1 cup grated natural Monterey Jack cheese

Saute' onion in butter 5 minutes. Add tomato and cook for 4 minutes. Stir in stock, oregano and wheat. Simmer 10 minutes. Add cheese and stir until melted.

Artichoke Soup (6 servings)

3 medium artichokes, split (chokes removed)
3½ cups Miso Broth (page 6)
4 lemons, thinly sliced
2 Tbsp. minced green onion
1 cup yogurt
Lemon slices

Cook artichokes in broth with lemon slices until artichokes are tender. Remove from heat; cool 2 hours. Discard lemon slices. Remove leaves from artichokes. Discard (or dip them in butter and eat them). Mash artichoke hearts and stems. Stir into broth. Stir in green onions and yogurt. Heat thoroughly. Serve with lemon slices. (If you desire a heartier appearing soup, mash two artichoke hearts and coarsely chopped the other. Add to soup.)

Black Bean Soup (serves 6)

4 lbs. black beans
1 cup butter
1 onion, chopped
2 carrots, chopped
2 cups celery, chopped
2 cups green pepper, chopped
3 cups Miso Broth (page 6)
1 tsp. mace
1 tsp. thyme

Wash beans. Soak overnight in water to cover. Add remaining ingredients to undrained beans; cover and simmer 5 hours. Cool slightly, then puree in blender or food mill. Reheat.

Brussels' Sprouts Soup (6 servings)

2 lbs. Brussels' sprouts
4 cups Rich Vegetable Broth (page 8)
2 cups carrot juice
4 medium potatoes, diced
1 Tbsp. minced dill
½ tsp. vegetable salt (optional)

Combine all ingredients in heavy saucepan or kettle. Simmer, covered, 20 minutes.

Butternut-Chestnut Soup (6 servings)

1 quart Miso Broth (page 6)
1 cup cubed butternut squash
1 onion, chopped
½ cup chopped celery
½ cup grated carrot
½ lb. chestnuts, boiled and shelled
2 bay leaves
1 cup raw milk
½ cup milk powder
2 tsp. soy flour
¼ cup minced parsley

Heat broth. Add vegetables, chestnuts and bay. Cover and simmer until vegetables are tender. Remove bay. Blend milk, milk powder and flour. Add to soup mixture; heat. Sprinkle with parsley.

Butternut Soup (6 servings)

1½ quarts whole milk
2 Tbsp. butter
½ cup whole wheat flour
3 cups cooked, mashed butternut squash
½ tsp. vegetable salt (optional)
Dash cayenne
¼ cup minced parsley
½ tsp. ground nutmeg

Melt butter in saucepan. Stir in flour. Slowly add milk, stirring constantly, until thickened.

Slowly stir in squash and seasonings. Cook, stirring, until soup has thickened and soup is heated through.

Cabbage and Beet Soup (6 to 8 servings)

1 head cabbage, shredded
3 cups cooked beets, diced
1 small onion, diced
1 quart Vegetable Bouillon (page 9)
1 quart carrot juice
¼ tsp. sea salt (optional)
1 cup fresh cranberries
¼ tsp. allspice
2 Tbsp. honey

Combine all ingredients and cook until cabbage is tender and cranberries have popped open.

Cabbage Borsch (8 servings)

2 lb. ripe tomatoes, chopped
4 cups shredded cabbage
3 cups water
1 cup chopped onion
1 tart apple, cored and chopped
4 vegetable bouillon cubes
1 Tbsp. honey
1 Tbsp. freshly squeezed lemon juice
¼ tsp. cayenne

Combine ingredients in kettle. Cover and simmer 25 minutes.

Cabbage-Rice Soup (3 servings)

3 cups Miso Broth (page 6)
¼ cup uncooked brown rice
1 cup shredded cabbage
1 Tbsp. butter
¼ cup grated natural cheese

Bring broth to boiling. Add rice and simmer until rice is cooked. Add butter and cabbage and cook 5 minutes. Stir in cheese. Serve immediately.

Caraway Soup (serves 5 to 6)

1½ Tbsp. whole caraway seeds
½ tsp. vegetable salt (optional)
6 cups boiling water
3 Tbsp. butter, melted
4 Tbsp. flour
½ cup yogurt
Whole wheat croutons

Combine seeds, salt and water. Cover and simmer 15 minutes.
Blend butter and flour. Add 2 cups to soup to butter mixture. Stir until smooth, then return to soup pot. Heat. Place yogurt in serving bowls. Pour soup over yogurt. Garnish with croutons.

Cauliflower Soup (4 servings)

1 tsp. dill
2 cups cooked cauliflower
1 Tbsp. butter
¼ tsp. vegetable salt (optional)
1 cup cooking liquid from cauliflower or other vegetable
1 cup onion, minced
1 cooked medium-sized potato, mashed
2 cups Rich Vegetable Broth (page 8)
½ cup grated natural Swiss cheese

Combine cauliflower with butter, salt, dill, liquid, onion, potato and broth. Heat to boiling. Place a couple of tablespoonfuls of cheese in each bowl. Spoon soup over cheese.

Corn-Lima Soup (serves 2)

1 cup fresh raw corn
1 cup fresh lima beans
2 Tbsp. chopped onion
2 ripe tomatoes, quartered
1 Tbsp. honey
¼ tsp. oregano

Whirl all ingredients in blender until ingredients have liquefied. Serve at room temperature.

Corn-Watercress Soup (6 servings)

1 Tbsp. minced parsley
1/8 tsp. dried marjoram
1 quart Vegetable Soup Base (page 10)
2 cups corn scraped from the cob
1 cup watercress, chopped
3 Tbsp. butter
Sea salt (optional)
2 hard-cooked eggs, sliced

Add parsley and marjoram to soup base and simmer 10 minutes. Add corn and simmer 15 minutes. Add watercress and butter to hot soup. Season with salt. Garnish with egg slices.

Curly Dock-Brown Rice Soup (serves 6)

6 Tbsp. brown rice
1 quart boiling water
1/4 tsp. sea salt (optional)
2 carrots, sliced
1 1/2 cups young curly dock greens, in bite-sized pieces
3 medium turnips, pared and cubed
1 cup chopped onion
1 Tbsp. butter
2 cups raw milk

Add rice to boiling water with salt added. Boil 5 minutes, then add vegetables. Simmer, uncovered, 20 minutes; cover and simmer an additional 10 minutes. Add butter and milk. Heat thoroughly, being careful not to boil.

Curried Fresh Pea Soup (serves 2)

1 cup fresh peas
1 onion, sliced
2 carrots, sliced
2 cloves garlic, crushed
½ cup chopped celery
1 potato, sliced
½ tsp. vegetable salt (optional)
2½ tsp. curry powder
2 cups Vegetable Bouillon (page 9)
1 cup yogurt

Mix ingredients in large bowl. Blend in blender, ½ at time, until smooth. Pour into saucepan and heat, stirring. Do not boil.

Dutch Carrot Soup (5 to 6 servings)

4 carrots, shredded
½ medium onion, minced
2 stalks celery, minced
¼ cup butter
5 cups Carrot-Spinach Broth (page 5)
3 Tbsp. farina
Dash cayenne
Dash mace (the spice, not the spray repellent)

Saute' vegetables in butter until onion is lightly browned. Add broth, farina and seasonings. Cover pot and simmer 20 minutes.

Duchess Soup with Dandelion Greens (serves 3)

1 cup young dandelion greens
1 Tbsp. butter
¼ cup minced onion
1 Tbsp. whole wheat flour
3 cups raw milk
2 Tbsp. natural Cheddar cheese, grated
2 egg yolks
¾ cup yogurt
¼ tsp. crushed celery seed

Boil greens in ½ cup water 10 minutes. Drain well. Melt butter in saucepan. Add onion and saute' 3 minutes. Blend in flour. Slowly stir in milk. Cook until mixture thickens slightly. Beat together cheese, yolks and yogurt. Add to soup along with greens. Season. Heat but do not boil. Serve at once.

East Indies Sprout Soup (6 servings)

1 tsp. grated ginger root
½ tsp. sea salt (optional)
2 quarts Clear Mushroom Stock (page 6)
3 onions, sliced
2 cups fresh mung bean sprouts
3 hard-cooked eggs, sliced
Lemon slices

Add ginger, salt and onions to stock and cook 3 minutes. Add sprouts and eggs just before serving. Garnish with lemon slices.

Eggplant Soup (3 to 4 servings)

1 medium-sized eggplant
1 vine-ripened tomato, chopped
3½ cups water
2 Tbsp. grated onion
1 tsp. celery seeds
½ tsp. sea salt (optional)
1 Tbsp. honey (optional)
¼ cup hulled millet
¼ cup grated carrot

Bake eggplant until tender. Cool.
Combine tomato with water, onion, celery seeds, salt, honey, millet and carrot in saucepan. Add a sprig of any herbs you may have growing around. Cover soup and simmer 25 to 30 minutes.
Peel and dice eggplant. Add to soup. Heat thoroughly before serving.

French Tomato Soup (6 servings)

2 medium-sized ripe tomatoes, chopped
2 carrots, grated
2 small potatoes, grated
4 cups water
1 Tbsp. butter
1 tsp. vegetable salt (optional)
1 tsp. dried tarragon
½ tsp. dried marjoram
⅛ tsp. cayenne
1 cup sour cream
Whole wheat croutons

Combine all ingredients, except sour cream and croutons, in kettle. Cover and simmer for 30 minutes. Stir in sour cream and heat, but do not boil. Serve with croutons.

Fresh Dill-Vegetable Soup (serves 4 to 5)

2 Tbsp. butter
2 onions, chopped
1 green pepper, chopped
2 cups shredded cabbage
1½ cups fresh green beans, sliced
3 sprigs dill, chopped
2 bay leaves
2 cups ripe tomatoes, chopped
4 cups raw milk
2 Tbsp. whole wheat flour

Lightly saute' onions, green pepper, cabbage and green beans in butter. Add herbs and tomatoes. Mix milk with flour. Blend into soup. Heat thoroughly (but do not boil).

Garlic Soup (5 to 6 servings)

8 cloves garlic, crushed
6 Tbsp. peanut oil
Dash cayenne
6 slices cubed whole wheat bread
6 cups water
1 tsp. sea salt (optional)
4 eggs, beaten
2 Tbsp. snipped parsley

Saute' garlic in oil until garlic softens. Add bread and brown lightly. Blend in water and salt. Cover and cook slowly for 25 minutes. Blend in eggs and cook 5 minutes longer. Garnish with parsley.

Garden Tomato Soup (4 servings)

2 cups carrot juice
6 large tomatoes, chopped
1 medium onion, chopped
2 carrots, grated
¼ cup minced parsley
2 tsp. chopped fresh dill
2 tsp. chopped fresh basil
2 Tbsp. honey or maple sugar
1 tsp. sea salt (optional)
Dash cayenne
2 Tbsp. freshly squeezed lemon juice

Put all ingredients, except lemon juice, in kettle. Bring to boiling. Reduce heat. Cover and simmer 45 minutes. Force soup through a coarse sieve. Add lemon juice, heat and serve. (May also be served chilled.)

Grandma's Vegetable Soup (4 servings)

¼ cup butter
1 celery heart, finely sliced
3 leeks, thinly sliced
1 medium onion, thinly sliced
½ tsp. vegetable salt (optional)
3 cups water
3 medium potatoes, grated
1½ cups shredded cabbage
1 carrot, grated
2 cups raw milk
2 cups whole wheat croutons

Saute' celery, leeks and onion in butter for 10 minutes. Add salt, water, potatoes, cabbage and carrots. Cover and cook over medium heat for 25 minutes. Add milk. Heat but do not boil. Divide croutons among bowls. Ladle hot soup over croutons.

Green Kern Soup (4 servings)

1/2 cup dried green wheat
4 cups water
1/4 cup minced parsley
1/2 cup minced celery
2 quarts water
1 1/2 cups **Dry Soup Mix** (page 4)
1 Tbsp. butter
1 Tbsp. flour
1/2 cup yogurt

Soak wheat in 4 cups water for 1 hour. Add parsley and celery. Cover and simmer 15 minutes. Add water and soup mix. Cover and simmer gently 1 1/2 hours.

Melt butter. Stir in flour. Slowly stir into soup. Bring to boiling. Stir in yogurt and serve.

Green Pea Soup (serves 4 to 6)

2 cups **Mushroom Broth** (page 7)
  or **Bran Broth** (page 5)
1 quart water
1 quart fresh raw green peas
1/2 cup diced celery
1 medium onion, diced
1 turnip, diced
1/4 cup chopped mint
1 Tbsp. whole wheat flour
1 Tbsp. butter
1/4 tsp. **sea salt** (optional)
Dash cumin

Reserve 1/2 cup peas. Add remaining peas to kettle along with broth, water, celery, onion, turnip and mint. Simmer until vegetables are tender-crisp.

Melt butter in skillet. Stir in flour. Add small amount of hot soup liquid to butter mixture and stir mixture into simmering soup. Cook until mixture is thickened. Add reserved peas. Season with salt and cumin.

Groats and Potato Soup (serves 6)

1½ quarts Tomato Bouillon (page 9)
 or Mushroom Broth (page 7)
5 cups cubed unpeeled raw potatoes
2 large onions, diced
¼ cup buckwheat groats
1 cup raw milk
¼ cup minced parsley
1½ tsp. fresh oregano
½ tsp. sea salt (optional)

Bring bouillon or broth to boiling. Add potatoes, onions and groats. Cover and simmer until potatoes are tender. Stir in milk and herbs. Simmer 5 minutes longer.

Herbed Potato Soup (6 servings)

4 medium potatoes, diced
2 medium onions, minced
3½ cups water
2 Tbsp. butter
2 Tbsp. minced parsley
½ tsp. crushed dried basil
¼ tsp. dill seed
2 Tbsp. whole wheat flour
½ tsp. vegetable salt (optional)
2 cups cold milk
2 cups scalded milk

Cook potatoes and onion in 3½ cups water until potatoes are tender. Cool slightly, then blend or mash well with liquid in which they were cooked.

Melt butter in large skillet and add seasonings. Blend in flour; gradually stir in cold milk. Add scalded milk. Cook, stirring, over medium heat until mixture thickens slightly. Stir into potato-onion mixture. Heat, but do not boil.

Herb Soup (4 servings)

½ cup carrot juice
2 ripe medium-sized tomatoes, chopped
⅔ cup chopped onion
1 carrot, grated
½ cup celery leaves
1 tsp. fresh basil, chopped
1 tsp. fresh tarragon
2 tsp. fresh parsley
1½ cups Miso Broth (page 6)

Combine all ingredients (except broth) in blender container and puree. Add to saucepan along with broth and heat to boiling.

Herbed Spinach Soup (6 to 8 servings)

3 green onions, sliced
¼ cup minced parsley
2 Tbsp. minced chives
1 cup shredded lettuce
1 cup torn spinach
2 Tbsp. butter
¼ tsp. sea salt (optional)
1 cup Dry Soup Mix (page 4)
6 cups water
Dash cayenne
½ tsp. dried tarragon
½ tsp. dried rosemary
½ cup yogurt

Combine all ingredients, except yogurt, in kettle. Cover and simmer 25 minutes. Stir in yogurt. Serve at once.

Hubbard Squash Soup (serves 5 to 6)

1 cup diced onion
½ cup chopped celery
2 Tbsp. butter
¼ cup whole wheat flour
3 cups milk
1 ½ cups cooked mashed hubbard squash
½ tsp. celery seed
½ tsp. curry powder
Chopped parsley

Saute' onion and celery in butter. Stir in flour. Slowly add milk, stirring. Continue to stir until mixture thickens. Add squash, celery seed and curry powder. Heat. Garnish with parsley.

Kohlrabi Soup (serves 4 to 6)

8 medium kohlrabi
3 Tbsp. butter
2 cups chopped onion
5 cups water
6 vegetable bouillon cubes
2 cups carrot juice
⅛ tsp. ground nutmeg

Remove stems and leaves from kohlrabi; tear enough tender inner leaves to make 3 cups. Set aside. Remove tough outer skin from bulbs. Cut bulbs into cubes.
Saute' onion in butter 3 minutes. Add kohlrabi and saute' 3 minutes longer. Add water, bouillon cubes and carrot juice. Cover and simmer 25 minutes. Whirl half the cooked kohlrabi and small amount of broth in blender until smooth. Return to soup. Add leaves. Simmer 2 minutes. Sprinkle with nutmeg before serving.

Leek and Potato Soup (serves 6)

6 leeks, cut in thin slices
3 Tbsp. butter
2½ cups diced potatoes
1 quart Clear Mushroom Broth (page 6)
1 tsp. vegetable salt (optional)
Dash cayenne
Dash nutmeg
2½ Tbsp. butter
2 Tbsp. whole wheat flour

Saute' leeks in 3 Tbsp. butter until soft. Add potatoes and broth and bring to boiling. Boil 2 minutes. Reduce heat and simmer 20 minutes. Add seasonings. Cool slightly, then puree in blender.

Melt butter in saucepan. Stir flour into melted butter. Add small amount of puree soup to flour mixture, then stir mixture into bulk of soup. Cook over moderate heat until mixture thickens.

Lemon-Rice Soup (serves 3)

3 vegetable bouillon cubes
3 cups boiling water
½ cup brown rice
4 beaten eggs
3 Tbsp. freshly squeezed lemon juice
2 tsp. grated lemon rind

Dissolve cubes in boiling water. Add rice. Cover and simmer 25 minutes. Remove from heat.

Combine eggs with lemon juice. Beat until frothy. Combine ½ cup broth with mixture, then add to pot. Add rind. Cook until heated, stirring constantly.

Marigold Soup (serves 4 to 6)

    4 cups Vegetable Soup Base (page 10)
    2 cups water
    1 cup carrot juice
    ½ onion, grated
    1 turnip, grated
    1 potato, grated
    2 cups cooked brown rice
    ½ cup marigold petals

Combine all ingredients except petals. Cover and simmer 20 minutes. Sprinkle petals over soup just before serving.

Millet-Vegetable Soup (serves 8)

    6 quarts Vegetable Stock (page 10)
    1½ cups millet
    2 cups fresh tomato puree'
    1 large onion, diced
    1 cup diced carrot
    ½ cup diced turnip
    ½ tsp. sea salt (optional)
    Dash cayenne

Add millet to stock; bring to boil and simmer over low heat 1 hour. Add vegetables and seasoning. Cover and simmer 30 minutes longer.

Mint Soup (serves 4)

1½ cups water
2 cloves garlic, crushed
3 Tbsp. fresh mint
½ tsp. chile powder
2 Tbsp. whole wheat flour
½ tsp. sea salt (optional)
4 cups Clear Mushroom Stock (page 6)

Put water, garlic, mint, chili powder, flour and salt in blender container. Whirl at high speed 20 seconds. Pour into saucepan. Add stock and heat to boiling.

Mushroom and Dill Soup (6 servings)

½ lb. mushrooms, sliced
3 Tbsp. butter
½ tsp. caraway seeds
½ tsp. paprika
1 Tbsp. whole wheat flour
4 cups Tomato Bouillon (page 9)
1 cup yogurt
2 Tbsp. chopped fresh dill

Saute' mushrooms in butter with caraway seeds and paprika for 1 minutes. Sprinkle with flour. Stir well. Slowly stir in bouillon. Cover and simmer for 10 minutes. Stir in yogurt and dill. Mix well. Serve at once.

Nettle Soup (serves 4 to 5)

1 quart stinging nettles (young greens)
5 cups Mushroom Broth (page 7)
½ cup cooked wheat or rice

Add nettles and wheat or rice to broth. Simmer 12 minutes. Season to taste.

Onion Soup (serves 6)

6 medium onions, chopped
5 Tbsp. butter
3 cups cold water
1 egg yolk, beaten
3 Tbsp. whole wheat flour
2 cups scalded raw milk
Sea salt (optional)
Cayenne
Grated natural Swiss cheese

Saute' onions in 2 Tbsp. butter. Add water and cook 30 minutes. Cool slightly; puree in blender or food mill. Return to heat.

Melt remaining butter in small skillet. Stir in flour. Add small amount of scalded milk to butter mixture, then stir into scalded milk. Simmer 5 minutes, stirring constantly. Add egg yolk and heat soup, but do not boil. Season. Serve topped with grated cheese.

Parsley and Rice Soup (5 to 6 servings)

3 Tbsp. safflower oil
1 medium onion, minced
3 medium potatoes, grated
1 cup minced parsley
2 quarts water
2 Tbsp. Dry Soup Mix (page 4)
¾ cup raw brown rice
3 Tbsp. butter
½ cup grated natural Swiss cheese

Saute' onion in oil until onion is golden brown. Add potatoes, parsley, water and soup mix. Bring to boiling; add rice and reduce heat. Simmer, covered, until rice is tender. Add butter and cheese. Serve at once.

Pea and Tomato Puree (5 to 6 servings)

½ lb. dried yellow split peas
1 pint ripe chopped tomatoes
1 quart water
1 medium onion, sliced
3 celery tops, minced
Sea salt (optional)
Cumin to taste
1 Tbsp. whole wheat flour
1 Tbsp. butter

Cover peas with 3 quarts water and allow them to soak overnight. Drain. Put drained peas in heavy saucepan or kettle along with tomatoes, water, onion and celery. Simmer over medium heat until peas are tender. Cool slightly, then force through sieve or puree in blender. Season with salt and cumin.

Melt butter in skillet. Stir in flour to form a paste. Add ½ cup pureed pea mixture to butter-flour mixture. Stir until smooth, that add to remaining soup. Heat to boiling.

Potato-Watercress Soup (3 to 4 servings)

2 Tbsp. butter
½ cup chopped green onion
2 cups shredded potato
2 cloves garlic, crushed
3 cups carrot juice
1½ cups packed watercress leaves
2 Tbsp. chopped parsley
¼ tsp. vegetable salt (optional)
½ cup yogurt

Saute' onions in butter. Add potato, garlic, carrot juice, watercress, parsley and salt. Simmer, covered, 20 minutes. Stir in yogurt. Serve at once.

Pumpkin Soup (4 servings)

2 cups water
½ cup Dry Soup Mix (page 4)
½ cup green pepper, diced
1 large tomato, diced
2 green onions, sliced
2 sprigs parsley, minced
¼ tsp. dried thyme
2 cups cubed cooked pumpkin
1 Tbsp. whole wheat flour
2 Tbsp. butter
1 cup raw milk
½ tsp. nutmeg
1 tsp. honey
¼ tsp. sea salt (optional)

Combine water, soup mix, green pepper, tomato, onions, parsley and thyme in kettle. Bring to boiling. Reduce heat and simmer 20 minutes. Add pumpkin and simmer 5 minutes.

Melt butter in skillet. Stir in flour. Slowly add milk. Stir in nutmeg, honey and salt. Add to simmering soup. Cook 3 minutes.

Purslane Soup (4 servings)

4 cups Miso Broth (page 6)
½ tsp. freshly grated ginger root
½ tsp. Tamari soy sauce
½ cup minced green onion
1 cup chopped purslane leaves

Heat together broth, ginger and soy sauce until simmering. Add green onions and simmer 1 minutes. Stir in purslane and serve at once.

Seaweed Soup (4 servings)

2 Tbsp. safflower oil
1 onion, thinly sliced
1 cup snow or sugar pea pods
1 tsp. freshly grated ginger root
1 Tbsp. Tamari soy sauce
3 cups Clear Mushroom Stock (page 6)
4 Strips roasted nori seaweed, crumbled

Cook onions and peas in oil for 5 minutes. Stir in remaining ingredients. Bring to boiling; reduce heat and simmer, covered, 7 to 8 minutes.

Sheppard's Purse-Herb Soup (serves 5 to 6)

¼ cup butter
2 cups young Sheppard's Purse greens, chopped
1 cup chopped watercress
2 Tbsp. minced parsley
6 cups boiling water
7 vegetable bouillon cubes
½ cup yogurt
1 egg yolk
Sea salt (optional)
Cayenne to taste
Whole wheat croutons

Saute' Sheppard's Purse, watercress and parsley in butter for 5 minutes. Add water and bouillon cubes. Cover and simmer slowly for 30 minutes. Mix yogurt with yolk. Stir into simmering soup. Season. Remove from heat and serve with croutons.

Spinach Soup (serves 4 to 5)

2 lbs. spinach leaves, chopped
½ cup minced onion
¼ cup butter
4 cups Vegetable Soup Base (page 10)
Yogurt

Cook spinach and onion in butter until spinach is wilted and onion is soft. Add to soup base and bring to boiling. Simmer 2 to 3 minutes. Serve garnished with a spoonful of yogurt.

Spring Asparagus Soup (serves 5 to 6)

3 Tbsp. butter
4 green onions, chopped
1 small onion, chopped
3 new potatoes, grated
1 carrot, grated
2 quarts water
¼ cup barley
12 stalks fresh asparagus, cut into 1" pieces
½ lb. spinach leaves, torn
1 cup yogurt

Saute' onion in butter until tender. Add potatoes, carrot and water. Cover; bring to boiling. Reduce heat and simmer for 5 minutes. Add barley and asparagus and simmer 25 minutes. Add spinach and simmer 5 minutes longer. Stir in yogurt just prior to serving.

String Bean Soup (6 servings)

2 large cloves garlic, crushed
1 sweet red pepper, cut into strips
1/4 cup safflower oil
2 lb. ripe tomatoes, chopped
1 lb. string beans, cut in 1" pieces
1/2 cup water
1 tsp. sea salt (optional)
1 1/2 Tbsp. minced fresh basil
30 small whole grain crackers

Saute' garlic and red pepper in oil for 3 to 4 minutes. Add tomatoes and cook 10 minutes. Add beans, water and salt. Cook over medium heat for 20 minutes. Divide basil and crackers among 6 bowls. Ladle hot soup over ingredients in bowls.

Summer Soup (serves 4)

1 quart water
1 tsp. vegetable salt (optional)
2 medium zucchini, chopped
2 cups chopped spinach
1/4 cup chopped onion
1/4 cup rye flour
2 Tbsp. soybean oil
1/4 cup minced parsley

Bring water to boiling; add salt, zucchini, spinach and onion. Cook 10 minutes. Blend flour with oil. Add small amount of soup mixture to flour mixture and stir until smooth. Add to remaining soup mixture and stir well. Top with parsley.

Tomato and Dill Soup (serves 2 to 3)

3 large ripe tomatoes, diced
1 medium onion, diced
2 cloves garlic, crushed
¼ tsp. sea salt (optional)
Dash cayenne
3 sprig fresh dill, chopped
1½ cups carrot juice
½ cup cooked brown rice
1 cup yogurt

Combine tomatoes, onion, garlic, salt, cayenne, dill and carrot juice in saucepan. Simmer gently 15 minutes. Add rice and yogurt. Heat, but do not boil. Serve at once.

Tomato Bisque (5 to 6 servings)

4 cups raw milk
¾ cup dry whole wheat bread crumbs
1 small onion stuck with 8 whole cloves
2 sprigs of parsley, minced
1 bay leaf
2 cups cooked tomatoes
1½ tsp. honey
3 Tbsp. butter
½ tsp. sea salt (optional)
Yogurt

Scald milk with bread crumbs, onion, parsley and bay. Remove cloves and bay. Put milk mixture in blender container along with tomatoes, butter, honey and salt. Puree. Pour mixture into saucepan and heat, but do not boil. Top individual bowlfuls with a spoonful of yogurt and serve at once.

Tomato-Potato Soup (4 servings)

6 ripe tomatoes, chopped
6 potatoes, diced
2 onions, diced
1 quarter water
½ red chili pepper, crushed
1 green pepper, diced
¼ cup minced parsley
1 cup carrot juice

Put tomatoes, potatoes, onions and water in kettle and simmer, covered 1 hour. Mash tomatoes and potatoes with fork and add remaining ingredients. Simmer 20 minutes longer.

Vegetable-Brown Rice Soup (serves 5)

½ cup brown rice
2 quarts water
1 tsp. vegetable salt (optional)
1 cup sliced green beans
1 cup chopped green tomatoes
1 cup chopped onion
2 Tbsp. soybean oil
2 tsp. chopped parsley
1 tsp. Tarmari soy sauce
1 tsp. fresh oregano

Boil rice in water until tender. Add remaining ingredients and cook until vegetables are tender-crisp. Serve at once.

Watercress-Lemon Soup (serves 4 to 6)

1 quart water
2 cups cubed potatoes
4 vegetable bouillon cubes
½ cup raw milk
¼ tsp. ground nutmeg
2 Tbsp. arrowroot starch
5 cups lightly packed torn watercress leaves
¼ cup freshly squeezed lemon juice

Combine water, potatoes and bouillon. Simmer, covered, 15 minutes.
Blend together milk, nutmeg and starch. Stir into potatoes. Simmer, stirring, until mixture thickens. Add watercress and cook 2 minutes. Stir in lemon juice.

Watercress Soup (serves 4)

4 cups Mushroom Broth (page 7)
¼ tsp. sea salt (optional)
½ tsp. honey
2 tsp. Tamari soy sauce
3 paper-thin sliced fresh ginger root
½ cup water
1 large bunch watercress, broken into sprigs
2 Tbsp. finely sliced green onions.

Combine broth, salt, honey, soy sauce, ginger and water. Simmer 15 minutes. Bring to a full boil and add watercress and green onions. Cover, reduce heat, and simmer 2 minutes.

West African Peanut Soup (4 servings)

3 Tbsp. butter
½ cup minced celery
1 medium onion, minced
2 Tbsp. whole wheat flour
1 cup raw milk
½ cup natural peanut butter
2 cups Clear Mushroom Stock (page 6)
½ cup ground raw peanuts

Saute' celery and onion in butter until onion is tender. Mix in flour. Remove from heat and slowly add milk. Cook over medium heat, stirring, until thickened. Add peanut butter, then stock. Heat without boiling. Sprinkle ground peanuts over each serving.

Yam Soup (4 to 6 servings)

1 lb. yams, peeled and sliced
1 medium onion, minced
3 cups water
3 Tbsp. butter
3 cups raw milk
1 tsp. sea salt (optional)
Dash allspice

Cook yams and onion in water for 25 minutes. Puree in blender or food mill. Add remaining ingredients, heat and serve at once.

Chapter 8

Dumplings, Noodles, Crackers and Soup Toppers

Butter Dumplings

2½ Tbsp. softened butter
2 eggs
6 Tbsp. whole wheat flour
⅛ tsp. sea salt (optional)

Beat together butter and eggs. Stir in flour and salt. Drop batter by teaspoonfuls into simmering soup. Simmer, covered, 8 minutes.

Cheese Balls

2 eggs, separated
3 Tbsp. grated natural Swiss cheese
2 Tbsp. dry whole wheat bread crumbs
¼ tsp. paprika
1 tsp. chopped parsley
Dash sea salt (optional)

Combine egg yolks, cheese, crumbs, paprika, parsley and salt.
Beat egg whites stiff, then fold into yolk-cheese mixture. Drop small spoonfuls into simmering soup. Simmer 1 to 2 minutes. Serve at once.

Cheese Dumplings

1½ cup whole wheat flour
1½ tsp. baking powder
1 egg
½ cup milk
¼ cup snipped parsley
3 Tbsp. grated natural Cheddar cheese

Comine ingredients in order given. Beat batter smooth. Drop by teaspoonfuls into simmering soup. Cook for 3 minutes; turn and cook 3 minutes longer.

Cornmeal Dumplings

2 cups cornmeal
½ tsp. sea salt (optional)
1½ Tbsp. soy flour
1 egg, beaten
Simmering soup
Whole wheat flour

Mix cornmeal and salt. Blend in egg. Pour enough soup over mixture to make a thick paste. Stir thoroughly. Form small balls. Dredge in flour. Drop balls into simmering soup. Cover and simmer 12 to 15 minutes.

Cracker Balls

1 egg, slightly beaten
2 Tbsp. butter, melted
1 Tbsp. milk
¼ tsp. vegetable salt (optional)
½ cup fine whole wheat cracker crumbs

Combine egg and butter; add remaining ingredients and mix thoroughly. Shape into tiny balls. Allow to stand 1 hour. Drop into simmering soup 15 minutes before soup has completely cooked.

Farina Dumplings

1 egg, lightly beaten
¼ tsp. vegetable salt (optional)
¼ cup farina
½ tsp. finely minced chives

Combine dumpling ingredients and drop by spoonfuls into simmering soup or broth. Simmer 10 minutes.

Nut Dumplings

⅔ cup ground raw cashews or walnuts
½ cup whole wheat bread crumbs
2 eggs, beaten
2 Tbsp. soy flour
3 Tbsp. wheat germ
2 Tbsp. raw milk
2 Tbsp. peanut oil
½ cup dry milk solids
¼ tsp. cinnamon (optional)

Combine all ingredients. Blend thoroughly. Form into walnut-sized balls. Drop balls into simmering soup; cover and simmer 15 minutes.

Potato Dumplings

1 cup cooked potatoes, mashed
½ cup whole wheat bread crumbs
½ cup wheat germ
2 Tbsp. oil
2 eggs, beaten
1 Tbsp. milk
½ cup milk powder
¼ tsp. powdered sage
¼ tsp. sea salt (optional)

Blend all ingredients. Dough will be firm. Shape into walnut-sized balls. Roll in additional wheat germ, if desired. Drop into simmering soup. Cover pot and simmer 4 to 5 minutes.

Rice Balls

1 cup cold cooked brown rice
2 Tbsp. whole wheat flour
1 egg, slightly beaten
Dash sea salt (optional)
Dash cayenne
Dash nutmeg
1 tsp. grated lemon rind
1½ tsp. minced dill

Rub rice through a sieve; add remaining ingredients and mix thoroughly. Form into marble-sized balls. Cook in simmering soup 15 to 20 minutes.

Saffron Dumplings

½ tsp. baking powder
1 cup whole wheat flour
Dash sea salt (optional)
½ cup butter
2 tsp. dried parsley
¼ cup milk
Pinch of powdered saffron

With pastry cutter or fingers, work butter into flour, salt and baking powder until mixture is the consistency of cornmeal. Heat parsley, milk and saffron together, then add to the flour and mix to make firm dough. Drop by teaspoonfuls into simmering soup. Cover and simmer 15 minutes.

Spinach Balls

1 cup cooked spinach, well drained and finely chopped
1 cup fine dry whole wheat bread crumbs
1 egg white
⅛ tsp. salt (optional)

Combine ingredients in mixing bowl. Allow to stand 20 to 25 minutes. Shape into marbe-sized balls. Add to simmering soup and cook 5 minutes.

Sponge Dumplings

½ cup raw milk
1 cup whole wheat flour
Dash sea salt (optional)
1 egg white
3 Tbsp. butter, melted
2 eggs yolks
2 egg whites, beaten stiff

Beat together milk, flour, salt and 1 egg white. Add butter and beat until mixture leaves sides of bowl. Beat in egg yolks 1 at a time. Fold in beaten whites. Eight minutes before soup is done, drop batter by teaspoonfuls into simmering soup. Cook 8 minutes.

Tamale Dumplings

¼ lb. grated natural Cheddar cheese
3 Tbsp. grated onion
1 tsp. chili powder
¾ cup cornmeal
½ cup whole wheat flour
1 tsp. baking powder
¼ tsp. sea salt (optional)
½ cup raw milk

In bowl, combine dry ingredients. Add milk and stir well. Stir in cheese and onion. Drop by spoonfuls into simmering soup. Cook to desired doneness.

Tomato Dumplings

1 cup whole wheat flour
1½ Tbsp. butter
1 Tbsp. grated natural Cheddar cheese
Dash ses salt (optional)
1 Tbsp. snipped parsley
⅓ cup tomato juice

Combine butter and flour using fingers or pastry cutter. Ad remaining ingredients and mix well. Add more juice if needed to make a thick batter. Drop by teaspoonfuls into simmering soup. Simmer 12 to 15 minutes.

Whole Wheat Dumplings

1 egg
1 Tbsp. butter, melted
⅓ cup raw milk
1 cup whole wheat flour
2 tsp. baking powder
½ tsp. vegetable salt (optional)

Beat egg; add butter and milk. Mix dry ingredients, then add to liquid. Beat well. Drop by teaspoonfuls into gently simmering soup. Cover tightly and cook 15 minutes.

Green Noodles

¼ lb. spinach leaves
2⅔ cup whole wheat flour
¼ tsp. sea salt (optional)
3 eggs

Cook spinach in small amount of water. Drain. Chop fine.
Place flour and salt in bowl. Add eggs, one at a time, mixing slightly after each addition. Add spinach and mix to make stiff dough. Turn dough onto lightly floured board and knead. Divide dough into halves. Roll each 1/8" thick. Cover with clean cloth and allow to stand 1 hour. Cut dough into stripes ¼" wide by 3" long. Allow to dry 3 to 4 hours. Store in tightly covered container.
When needed, cook in simmering soup 15 to 20 minutes.

Soy Noodles

1 cup soy flour
½ tsp. powdered vegetable bouillon
1 egg, beaten
3 Tbsp. raw milk

Blend flour, bouillon, egg and milk. Knead on lightly floured board. Chill 2 hours. Roll out thin. Allow to dry 15 minutes.
Cut into thin strips with sharp knife. Drop into simmering soup and allow to cook 10 to 15 minutes. If noodles are not to be used at once, dry thoroughly, then store in tightly covered container.

Spaetzle

2 eggs, well beaten
1¼ cup whole wheat flour
½ cup water
¼ tsp. sea salt (optional)
¼ tsp. baking powder

Combine ingredients and beat well. Push batter through a colander over simmering soup. Simmer 8 minutes.

Whole Wheat Noodles

3 egg yolks
1 egg
4 Tbsp. cold water
1 tsp. vegetable salt (optional)
2 cups whole wheat pastry flour

Beat egg yolks until very light in color. Add egg and beat again. Beat in water and salt. Using hands, work in flour. Divide dough into 3 parts. Roll each as thinly as possible on lightly floured board. Cover with towel until partially dry. Roll up jelly roll fashioned and cut into desired noodle width with sharp knife. Shake out noodles. Allow to dry. Store in covered container. Add dried noodles to simmering soup and simmer gently 15 to 20 minutes.

Chewy Whole Wheat Bread Sticks

1 package active dry yeast
1½ cups warm water
1 Tbsp. honey
5 cups whole wheat flour (approximately)
Melted butter
Granulated garlic

Sprinkle yeast over warm water; stir to dissolve. Stir in honey. Gradually beat in 3 cups flour. Beat well. Gradually add enough remaining flour to make a soft dough. Knead on lightly floured board until smooth and elastic, adding more flour if necessary. Divide dough into 32 equal pieces. Roll each into 10" long rope; arrange each 1" apart on greased baking sheets. Let rise in warm place for 15 minutes.

Lightly brush each rope with butter. Sprinkle with granulated garlic. Bake in preheated 400°F. oven for 15 minutes.

Millet Crackers

    1 package active dry yeast
    ½ cup lukewarm water
    ½ cup boiling water
    1 cup sunflower seed meal
    1 cup safflower oil
    3 cups millet flour
    1 cup whole wheat flour
    ¼ cup soy flour
    ¼ tsp. vegetable salt (optional)

    Soften yeast in lukewarm liquid. Pour boiling water over sunflower meal. Allow to stand 10 minutes. Combine yeast with sunflower mixture. Stir in oil, salt and flours. Work into stiff dough. Roll out on floured board. Cut into squares. Place squares on greased cookie sheet. Allow to rest for 10 minutes, then bake in preheated 250°F. oven for 30 minutes.

Rye Crackers

    2 cups rye flour
    ½ tsp. sea salt (optional)
    ¼ tsp. baking powder
    ¼ cup butter
    1 Tbsp. caraway seeds, crushed
    Cold water
    Sea or vegetable salt (optional)

    Sift together flour, salt and baking powder. Work in butter and seeds with pastry cutter or fingers, then add enough cold water to make a kneadable dough. Knead on floured board until smooth and elastic.
    Divide dough in half and roll each out as thinly as possible on floured board. Cut into 2" squares and place each on greased cookie sheet. Prick with fork, sprinkle with salt and bake in preheated 350°F. oven until lightly browned and crisp (10 to 12 minutes).

Sunflower Crackers (2 dozen)

2½ cups whole wheat flour
1 Tbsp. honey
¼ tsp. sea salt (optional)
½ tsp. baking powder
1¼ cups yogurt
1 egg, beaten
½ cup sunflower seeds

Combine all ingredients in mixing bowl. Mix until flour is evenly moistened. Turn onto lightly floured board and knead until mixture holds together in a smooth ball. Divide into 24 pieces. Roll each into a ball, then roll each into a 5" round. Bake on lightly greased cookie sheet at 400°F. 12 to 15 minutes.

Whole Wheat Crackers

2 cups whole wheat pastry flour
⅓ cup gluten flour
½ cup cracked wheat
⅓ cup corn oil
1 Tbsp. safflower oil
1 cup raw milk

Combine flours and cracked wheat. Add remaining ingredients all at once. Knead dough on lightly floured board. Roll out dough and cut into squares or desired shapes. Place on oiled cookie sheet; pierce each cracker with fork and bake at 250°F. for 1 hour.

Whole Wheat Sticks

2½ cups whole wheat pastry flour
½ cup cracked wheat
⅔ cup raw milk
¼ cup honey
2 Tbsp. safflower oil

Combine flour, cracked wheat, milk, honey and oil. Knead until smooth. Add a little more flour if dough is too sticky. Toss onto floured board. Roll in rope ½ inch thick. Cut rope into 4" lengths. Bake at 350°F. 8 to 10 minutes.

Cashew Balls

1 egg yolk
½ cup ground raw cashews
Dash sea salt (optional)
¼ tsp. grated lemon rind
1 egg white, beaten stiff
Safflower or peanut oil

Beat together yolk, cashews, salt and rind. Fold in egg white. Drop batter by teaspoonfuls into hot oil. Cook until golden. Add to soup just before serving.

Egg Balls

5 eggs
⅛ tsp. cayenne
1 tsp. vegetable salt (optional)
Whole wheat flour
Butter or safflower oil

Hard-cook 4 eggs, shell and mash yolks to a smooth paste. Add salt and pepper and raw egg. Mix well. Shape into tiny balls and roll then in whole wheat flour.

Heat butter or oil in skillet; saute' flour coated balls a few at a time, until lightly browned. Float egg balls in bowls of soup.

Soup Toppers

Grated natural cheese	Minced celery tops
Cubed tofu	Grated carrots
Sunflower seeds	Chopped chives
Wheat germ	Nasturtium flowers
Dab of yogurt	Mint leaves
Alfalfa sprouts	Radish slices
Radish sprouts	Grated coconut
Whole wheat croutons	Grated turnips
Toasted soybeans	Grated raw beets
Riced hard-cooked eggs	Chopped fresh herbs
Slivered almonds	Thin slices lemon
Chopped raw cashews	Piñyon nuts
Minced parsley	Marigold petals

Index

Page

A

Acorn Squash Soup 86
African Peanut Soup, West 114
Almond Soup, Cream of 17
Alpine Soup 86
Apple Bouillon 57
Apple Soup, Chilled 59
Apricot-Raspberry Soup, Fresh 62
Artichoke, Cream of 38
Artichoke Soup 87
Asparagus Chowder 25
Asparagus Soup, Cream of 38
Asparagus Soup, Spring 109
Austrian Potato Soup 37
Autumn Minestrone 67
Autumn Pear Soup 57
Autumn Vegetable Chowder 25
Avocado, Cream of 17
Avocado Soup, Hot Cream of 55
Avocado Soup, Mexican 78
Avocado-Spinach Soup 23
Avocado, Watercress Soup 23

B

Banana-Coconut Soup 58
Barley-Mushroom Soup 68
Base, Vegetable Soup 10
Bean and Basil Soup, White Kidney 85
Bean Porridge 69
Bean Soup, Dutch 74
Bean Soup, String 110
Beet-Potato Soup 11
Beet Soup, Cabbage 89
Beet Soup, Cream of 39
Bing Cherry Soup 58
Black Bean Soup 69

Black Soybean Soup 70
Borsh, Cabbage 90
Borsh, Iced 18
Bouillon, Apple 57
Bouillon, Orange 64
Bouillon, Potato-Vegetable 8
Bouillon, Tomato 9
Bouillon, Vegetable 9
Bouquet, Kitchen 4
Bran Broth 5
Bread Casserole Soup, Egg- 75
Bread Soup, Wheat 85
Broccoli-Cheese Soup 70
Broccoli Soup, Cream of 40
Broccoli Soup, Iced 19
Broth, Bran 5
Broth, Carrot-Spinach 5
Broth, Miso 6
Broth, Mushroom 7
Broth, Onion-Garlic 7
Broth, Rich Vegetable 8
Brown Rice-Fresh Pea Soup 71
Brown Rice Soup, Curly Dock 92
Brussel's Sprouts Soup 88
Butter Dumplings 115
Butternut-Chestnut Soup 88
Butternut Soup 89

C

Cabbage-Beet Soup 89
Cabbage-Rice Soup 90
Cabbage Soup, Cream of 41
Caraway Soup 90
Carrot-Cheese Soup 37
Carrot Soup, Cream of 41
Carrot Soup, Dutch 93
Carrot-Spinach Broth 5
Carrot-Turnip Stock 5
Cashew Balls 125
Cauliflower Soup 91
Cauliflower Soup, Cream of 42
Celery Chowder 26
Celery Soup, Cream of 42
Celery Soup, Cream of Onion and 47

Chard-Lentil Soup	77
Chard Soup, Lentil-	77
Cheddar Cheese Soup	71
Cheddar Chowder, Onion-	32
Cheese Balls	115
Cheese Chowder	26
Cheese Chowder, Corn and	27
Cheese Chowder, Potato-	33
Cheese Dumplings	116
Cheese Soup, Broccoli-	70
Cheese Soup, Carrot-	37
Cheese Soup, Mozzarella	79
Cheese Soup, Vegetable-	84
Chestnut Soup, Butternut	88
Chestnut Soup, Cream of	43
Chewy Whole Wheat Bread Sticks	122
Chickpea-Pasta Soup	72
Chickweed-Nettle Soup, Chilled	12
Chicory Soup, Cream of	43
Chilled Chickweed-Nettle Soup	12
Chilled Cream of Tomato Soup	12
Chilled Curried Soup	13
Chilled Herb Soup	13
Chilled Minestrone	14
Chilled Raspberry Soup	59
Chilled Salad Soup	14
Chilled Spinach Soup	15
Chilled Split Pea and Mint Soup	15
Chilled Strawberry-Rhubarb Soup	59
Chowder, Asparagus	25
Chowder, Autumn Vegetable	25
Chowder, Celery	26
Chowder, Cheese	26
Chowder, Corn	27
Chowder, Corn and Cheese	27
Chowder, Corn-Tomato	28
Chowder, Dried Corn	28
Chowder, Fiddlehead	29
Chowder, Green Chili and Corn	29
Chowder, Lima Bean	30
Chowder, New England Vegetable	30
Chowder, Oatmeal	31
Chowder, Okra	31

Chowder, Onion-Cheddar 32
Chowder, Parsnip................................. 32
Chowder, Potato 33
Chowder, Potato-Cheese 33
Chowder, Potato-Corn 34
Chowder, Soybean................................. 34
Chowder, Soya-Macaroni 35
Chowder, Tomato 35
Chowder, Tomato-Lima Bean 36
Chowder, Wheatberry 36
Citrus-Yogurt Soup 60
Coconut Soup 16
Coconut Soup, Banana-............................ 58
Coconut Soup, Curry 61
Cold Cucumber-Potato Soup 16
Cold Tomato-Yogurt Soup 17
Consomme', Jellied 20
Corn-Cheese Chowder.............................. 27
Corn Chowder 27
Corn Chowder, Dried 28
Corn Chowder, Potato-............................ 34
Corn-Lima Soup 91
Cornmeal Soup 72
Corn Minestrone, Cracked 73
Corn Soup, Cream of 44
Corn-Tomato Chowder 28
Corn Tortilla Soup 73
Corn-Watercress Soup 92
Cracked Corn Minestrone 73
Cracker Balls 116
Crackers, Millet.................................123
Crackers, Rye....................................123
Crackers, Sunflower 124
Crackers, Whole Wheat 124
Cream of Almond Soup 17
Cream of Asparagus Soup 38
Cream of Artichoke Soup 38
Cream of Avocado Soup 17
Cream of Avocado Soup, Hot....................... 55
Cream of Barley Soup 39
Cream of Beet Soup............................... 39
Cream of Broccoli Soup 40
Cream of Cabbage Soup............................ 41
Cream of Carrot Soup 41

Cream of Cauliflower Soup 42
Cream of Celery Soup 42
Cream of Chestnut Soup 43
Cream of Chicory Soup 43
Cream of Corn Soup 44
Cream of Cucumber Soup 44
Cream of Green Bean Soup 45
Cream of Jerusalem Artichoke Soup 45
Cream of Lettuce Soup 46
Cream of Lima Soup 46
Cream of Mushroom Soup 47
Cream of Onion and Celery Soup 47
Cream of Onion Soup 48
Cream of Peanut Butter Soup 48
Cream of Potato Soup 49
Cream of Potato Soup, Sour 55
Cream of Potato Soup, Swiss 56
Cream of Pumpkin Soup 49
Cream of Purslane Soup 50
Cream of Sorrel Soup 50
Cream of Soybean Soup 50
Cream of Spinach Soup 51
Cream of Squash Soup 51
Cream of Tomato Soup 52
Cream of Tomato Soup, Chilled 12
Cream of Turnip Soup 52
Cream of Vegetable Soup 53
Cream of Zucchini Soup 54
Cucumber-Mint Soup 18
Cucumber-Potato Soup 16
Cucumber Soup, Cream of 44
Cucumber Soup, Yogurt 24
Curried Fruit Soup 60
Curried Soup, Chilled 13
Curried Watercress Soup 54
Curry-Coconut Soup 61
Curry Soup, Indian 19
Curry Soup, Lentil 77

D

Dill Soup, Mushroom 104
Dill Soup, Tomato and 111
Dill-Vegetable Soup, Fresh 96
Dried Corn Chowder 28

Dried Fruit-Elderberry Soup 61
Dried Fruit Soup 62
Dry Soup Mix 4
Dumplings, Butter 115
Dumplings, Cheese 116
Dumplings, Cornmeal 116
Dumplings, Farina 117
Dumplings, Nut 117
Dumplings, Potato 117
Dumplings, Saffron 118
Dumplings, Sponge 119
Dumplings, Tamale 119
Dumplings, Tomato 120
Dumplings, Whole Wheat 120
Dutch Bean Soup 74
Dutch Carrot Soup 93
Duchess Soup with Dandelion Greens 94
Dutch Vegetable Soup 74

E

East Indies Sprout Soup 94
Egg Balls 125
Egg-Bread Casserole Soup 75
Eggplant Soup 95
Egg Soup 75
Elderberry Soup, Dried Fruit 61

F

Farina Dumplings 117
Fiddlehead Chowder 29
French Tomato Soup 95
Fresh Apricot-Pineapple Soup 62
Fresh Dill-Vegetable Soup 96
Fresh Pea Soup, Brown Rice 71
Fresh Prune Soup 63
Fresh Rosehip Soup 63
Fresh Vegetable Garden Soup 76
Fruit Soup, Curried 60
Fruit Soup, Dried 62

G

Garden Fresh Vegetable Soup 76
Garden Tomato Soup 97

Garlic Broth, Onion- 7
Garlic Soup 96
Grandma's Vegetable Soup 97
Grape Soup, Green 63
Green Bean Soup, Cream of. 45
Green Chili and Corn Chowder. 29
Green Grape Soup 63
Green Kern Soup 98
Green Noodles 121
Green Pea Soup 98
Groats and Potato Soup 99

H

Herbed Potato Soup 99
Herbed Spinach Soup. 100
Herb Soup 100
Herb Soup, Chilled. 13
Hot Cream of Avocado Soup 55
Hubbard Squash Soup 101

I

Iced Borsch 18
Iced Broccoli Soup 19
Indian Curry Soup 19

J

Jellied Consomme' 20
Jellied Tomato Soup. 20
Jellied Vegetable Soup 21
Jerusalem Artichoke Soup, Cream of 45

K

Kidney Bean and Basil Soup, White 85
Kitchen Bouquet. 4
Kohlrabi Soup 101

L

Leek and Potato Soup 102
Lemon-Rice Soup 102
Lemon Tree Soup 21
Lentil-Chard Soup 77
Lentil-Curry Soup. 77
Lentil Soup, Chard- 11

Lettuce Soup, Cream of 46
Lima Bean Chowder................................... 30
Lima Bean Chowder, Tomato- 36
Lima Soup, Corn- 91
Lima Soup, Cream of 46

M

Macaroni Chowder, Soya- 35
Marigold Soup 103
Meatless Minestrone 79
Melon Soup 64
Mexican Avocado Soup 78
Milk Soup, Sour 22
Millet Crackers 123
Millet-Vegetable Soup................................ 103
Minestrone, Autumn.................................. 67
Minestrone, Chilled 14
Minestrone, Cracked Corn 73
Minestrone, Meatless 79
Minestrone, Springtime............................... 83
Mint Soup 104
Mint Soup, Chilled Split Pea and 15
Mint Soup, Cucumber 18
Miso Broth 6
Mix, Dry Soup 4
Mozzarella Cheese Soup.............................. 79
Mushroom-Barley Soup............................... 80
Mushroom-Dill Soup 104
Mushroom-Noodle Soup 80
Mushroom Soup, Barley-.............................. 68
Mushroom Soup, Cream of 47
Mushroom Stock, Clear 6
Mushroom Soup with Tofu 81

N

Nettle Soup 104
Nettle Soup, Chilled Chickweed- 12
New England Vegetable Chowder..................... 30
Noodles, Green 121
Noodles Soup, Mushroom-............................ 80
Noodles, Whole Wheat................................ 122
Nut Dumplings 117

134

O

Okra Chowder 31
Oatmeal Chowder 31
Onion and Celery Soup, Cream of 47
Onion-Cheddar Chowder 32
Onion-Garlic Broth 7
Onion Soup 105
Onion Soup, Cream of 48
Orange Bouillon 64
Orange Soup 64

P

Parsley and Rice Soup 105
Parsnip Chowder 32
Pasta Soup, Chickpea- 72
Peach Soup 65
Peanut Butter Soup, Cream of 48
Peanut Soup, West African 114
Pear Soup, Autumn 57
Pea Soup, Curried Fresh 93
Pea and Tomato Puree 106
Pineapple Soup 65
Pineapple Soup, Strawberry 66
Piñyon Nut Soup 81
Potato-Cheese Chowder 33
Potato Chowder 33
Potato-Corn Chowder 34
Potato Dumplings 117
Potato Soup, Austrian 37
Potato Soup, Beet 11
Potato Soup, Cold Cucumber- 16
Potato Soup, Cream of 49
Potato Soup, Groats and 99
Potato Soup, Herbed 99
Potato Soup, Leek 102
Potato Soup, Sour Cream 55
Potato Soup, Swiss Cream of 56
Potato Soup, Tomato- 112
Potato-Vegetable Bouillon 8
Potato-Watercress Soup 106
Prune Soup, Fresh 63
Prune Soup, Rosehip- 65
Pumpkin Soup 107
Pumpkin Soup, Cream of 49

Purslane Soup 107
Purslane Soup, Cream of 50

Q

Quebec Pea Soup 82

R

Raspberry Soup, Chilled 59
Raspberry Soup, Fresh Apricot 62
Rhubarb Soup, Chilled Strawberry- 59
Rich Vegetable Broth 8
Rice Balls 118
Rice(brown)-Fresh Pea Soup 71
Rice(brown) Soup, Cabbage- 90
Rice(brown) Soup, Lemon- 102
Rice(brown) Soup, Parsley and 105
Rice(brown) Soup, Vegetable 112
Rosehip-Prune Soup 65
Rosehip Soup, Fresh 63
Rye Crackers 123

S

Saffron Dumplings 118
Salad Soup, Chilled 114
Seaweed Soup 108
Senegalese Soup 22
Sheppard's Purse-Herb Soup 108
Sorrel Soup, Cream of 50
Soup Mix, Dry 4
Sour Milk Soup 22
Soya-Macaroni Chowder 35
Soybean Chowder 34
Soybean-Vegetable Soup 82
Soybean Soup, Cream of 50
Soy Noodles 121
Spaetzle 121
Spinach-Avocado Soup 23
Spinach Balls 118
Spinach Soup 109
Spinach Soup, Chilled 15
Spinach Soup, Cream of 51
Spinach Soup, Herbed 100
Split Pea and Mint Soup, Chilled 15
Split Pea Soup 83

Sponge Dumplings 119
Squash Soup, Cream of 51
Springtime Minestrone 83
Sprout Soup, East Indies 94
Strawberry-Pineapple Soup 66
Strawberry-Rhubarb Soup, Chilled 59
String Bean Soup 110
Summer Soup 110
Sunflower Crackers 124

T

Tamale Dumplings 119
Tofu, Mushroom Soup with 81
Tomato Bisque 111
Tomato Bouillon 9
Tomato Chowder 35
Tomato Chowder, Corn 28
Tomato and Dill Soup 111
Tomato Dumplings 120
Tomato-Lima Bean Chowder 36
Tomato Soup, Chilled Cream of 12
Tomato Soup, Cream of 52
Tomato Soup, French 95
Tomato Soup, Garden 97
Tomato Soup, Jellied 20
Tomato-Yogurt Soup, Cold 17
Turnip Soup, Cream of 52
Turnip Stock, Carrot- 5

V

Vegetable Bouillon, Potato 8
Vegetable Broth Rich 8
Vegetable-Brown Rice Soup 84
Vegetable-Cheese Soup 84
Vegetable Chowder, Autumn 25
Vegetable Chowder, New England 30
Vegetable, Garden Fresh 76
Vegetable-Rice Soup 84
Vegetable Soup, Barley- 68
Vegetable Soup Base 10
Vegetable Soup, Cream of 53
Vegetable Soup, Dutch 74
Vegetable Soup, Fresh Dill- 96
Vegetable Soup, Grandma's 97

Vegetable Soup, Jellied 21
Vegetable Soup, Millet- 103
Vegetable Soup, Soybean 82
Vegetable Stock 10

W

Watercress-Avocado Soup 23
Watercress Soup 113
Watercress Soup, Corn 92
Watercress Soup, Cream of 53
Watercress Soup, Curried 54
Watercress Soup, Potato- 106
West African Peanut Soup 114
Wheatberry Chowder 36
Wheat Bread Soup 85
White Kidney Bean and Basil Soup 85
Whole Wheat Bread Sticks, Chewy 122
Whole Wheat Crackers 124
Whole Wheat Dumplings 120
Whole Wheat Noodles 122
Whole Wheat Sticks 124

Y

Yam Soup 114
Yogurt Soup, Citrus- 60
Yogurt Soup, Cold Tomato- 17
Yogurt-Cucumber Soup 24

Z

Zucchini Soup, Cream of 54